Shelf Life

To: Fred Gregory

with our Best wishes

AJ & Jimmy

10/17/07

Shelf Life

**HOW AN UNLIKELY ENTREPRENEUR
TURNED $500 INTO $65 MILLION
IN THE GROCERY INDUSTRY**

A. J. Scribante

Founder of MAJERS Corporation

Since 1947
**REGNERY
PUBLISHING, INC.**
An Eagle Publishing Company • Washington, DC

Library of Congress Cataloging-in-Publication Data

Scribante, A.J.
  Shelf life : how an unlikely entrepreneur turned $500 into $65 million in the grocery industry / A.J. Scribante.
    p. cm.
  ISBN 0-89526-025-5
  1. Scribante, A.J. 2. Businessmen—United States—Biography. 3. Grocery trade—Management. 4. Entrepreneurship. I. Title.
  HC102.5.S37A3 2005
  381'.41092—dc22

                                                                2005030661

Published in the United States by
Regnery Publishing, Inc.
One Massachusetts Avenue, NW
Washington, DC 20001

www.regnery.com

Distributed to the trade by
National Book Network
Lanham, MD 20706

Manufactured in the United States of America

10 9 8 7 6 5 4 3 2 1

Books are available in quantity for promotional or premium use. Write to Director of Special Sales, Regnery Publishing, Inc., One Massachusetts Avenue NW, Washington, DC 20001, for information on discounts and terms or call (202) 216-0600.

TABLE OF CONTENTS

ACKNOWLEDGMENTS

I have walked with love and support from three people who though now gone, are not forgotten: my mother, Mary, my father, Otto, and my brother, Otto, Jr. The endless gifts they gave to me became the bedrock for my success.

To the many highly respected employees of the MAJERS Corporation: Your exceptional talents, dedication, and hard work have made my dream become a reality. Thank you.

To all of my friends, suppliers, associates, and mentors: Our success is due to your endless support.

To the valued and revered team of the MAJERS outside Board of Directors: You guided our corporation with great wisdom, direction, advice, and compassion. A sincere thanks.

To our valued clients who made it all possible and who opened their minds to what could be possible with the implementation of MAJERS Customer Service: We couldn't have done it without you.

To the Omaha community and to the SAC Consultation Committee for your embrace and support while providing special opportunities with our military forces: We're proud to have made your great city our home and headquarters.

To the many individuals who touched my life in a positive way along this wonderful journey and also provided learning and growth in what became a fun and unique experience.

To the special talents of writer Mark Seal: You helped me put my story in order and give it life. Thanks, Mark.

Finally, to the great country we live in and its endless opportunities. God bless America.

INTRODUCTION

"Chase perfection, and settle for excellence along the way."
—Vince Lombardi

They call me, even now.

I'm supposed to be relaxing, enjoying retirement in my adopted hometowns of Aspen/Snowmass, Colorado, and Sanibel Island, Florida. But I'm constantly jolted from sleep and pulled from revelry by the call of an endless stream of empty shelves. They have one commandment: Fill me.

"Go back to sleep, Adie," my wife Sunny will say. "You've filled enough shelves to last six lifetimes." She's right, of course. My forty-year business career was a multi-faceted adventure with one constant—an exercise in filling shelves: ranging from personally selling household products, from bakery goods to bleach, and beyond, to creating MAJERS, a national marketing firm that helped America's top corporations move their products more efficiently and profitably through the shelves of America's supermarkets. In 1989 I sold MAJERS for $65 million and set about the good life of retirement.

But the shelves keep calling.

I began giving speeches to business groups, universities, on television, and at ceremonies. I tried to impart the things that I'd learned, talking about mission statements, courage in the face of rejection, the importance of principles, building an organization, dealing with risks and temporary failures.

A few years ago, it got the best of me. I pulled out a pen and pad and started stocking shelves anew: this time not with products, but with information, stories, memories. I discovered an insatiable need to pass on what I had learned, to tell the story of my unbelievable journey from corner grocery store to national chains to the biggest corporations in America. And while it's the story of only one man's business track, my goal in writing it is to show how what I learned can be applied to anybody and any business.

The title refers not only to my business timing—getting in and getting out of various enterprises at precisely the right time—but also to the arena in which I worked. In all of these various fields of endeavor, I learned that everything has a shelf life: bleach, groceries, and, of course, men. Only the lessons I learned and the improbable successes I achieved never expire. They are as applicable today as when they happened.

Herewith, *Shelf Life*, the story of an amazing business journey taken one improbable step at a time, filling one shelf, then another, until, incredibly, the shelves of my many disparate businesses led me to a destination I wouldn't have dreamed possible.

The story begins, fittingly, in the middle of nowhere....

THE SHELF OF

The Midwest Work Ethic

When I think of my birthplace of Osage City, Kansas, I see a little speck of light on an otherwise empty prairie. Osage is thirty-six miles south of Topeka and forty-five miles from Emporia, home of Emporia Teacher's College.

I see my father, Otto Joseph Scribante, dusted with the flour of his occupation as a baker, a trade he learned in the navy. He was convinced that he didn't need an education to be a baker, conventional thought in those days when quitting school for work was a common career move. The reason was simple survival; most families, including my father's, needed another hand to bring in money. But despite the lack of a formal education, Dad had a sophistication about him. He would dress in finery when the occasion demanded and proudly wore his diamond stickpin and solid-gold cufflinks emblazoned with his initials. He'd had them made in China, where he'd visited during his eight years in the service. His own father, who had been an interpreter on the docks in New Orleans, spoke seven languages and no doubt gave his son some of his sophistication.

Dad was an outgoing businessman and well-respected by associates in his profession. His personality and knowledge of the baking business allowed him to network his way into several managerial and ownership positions throughout the Midwest. Each year, the Seibel Institute of Baking Association would hold a conference at the Edgewater Beach Hotel in Chicago, attracting baking professionals from across the country, and there he would learn about opportunities for better jobs and openings.

In order to stay employed in those days, Dad was forced to move our family each time a better opportunity arose. It was an era filled with uncertainty, but rather than fretting about the circumstances, my father would pack his flour-dusted kids and wife into our car and follow the dream of a more stable future. He was a proud and independent man, firmly opinionated and ever-conscious of his duty to his family. What resulted for my brother and I was somewhat of a migratory childhood, our family relocating new towns every two to three years.

My father prided himself on his independence and worked as a bakery manager and flour salesman well-past retirement age. To him matters were either black or white and when he knew he was right he was firm in his belief. This attitude cost him a couple of manager jobs in places like Manhattan, Kansas, and Chicago, Illinois. But when one job didn't work out for one reason or another, he would more than likely hit the road with two flour-dusted kids and a wife in tow, always optimistic that he would find a better future for his family.

Though we were young, the moves were hard on my brother and I. Each new town meant making new friends and settling in yet again, if only for a short time. We used to spend hours making model airplanes but would have to leave them behind each time we moved since they wouldn't fit in the car. That kind of uncertainty can be hard for a child, but I learned early on how to reach out to strangers and make friends easily, a skill that has been an asset to me ever since.

The bakeries that my father managed or owned were extremely modest operations, mostly bare-bones places serving basic bread, cinnamon rolls, cakes, cookies, and simple essentials. But to us, the bakeries were our rock.

During the Depression, when most men were out of work, my father, the baker, lost only one job. Seeking better opportunities in his chosen field, he sold the bakery in Osage City and moved first to a large bakery plant in Manhattan, Kansas, then to another in Jackson, Michigan, and then to Kalamazoo. After that it was on to Chicago where he managed the bakery facility in the National-Tea grocery chain. He then bought his own bakery in Monet, Missouri, where we found a home for a while. Eventually we ended up back in Osage City, where he and my mother had lived just after they got married.

My mother was a farm girl, born in Fostoria, another little speck of light fifteen miles outside of Osage. Her father was a coal miner, and she was the youngest of four girls. Today, I can still hear my mother's laugh and can remember her strength. Like my dad, she dropped out of school in the seventh grade, but had some sort of natural intelligence and perseverance. Raising two active, growing boys and supporting my father in our many moves were duties she handled with strength and grace. We may have never stayed long in one place, but she kept us busy in various activities no matter where we lived, never letting an uncertain future interfere with our development. Being a supporting wife was as important to the survival of our family as my dad's ability to earn a wage.

When I was born in Osage City in 1930, about two thousand people called it home. Today, the population has grown to just over three thousand, a typical small town in the American Midwest. Settled after the Civil War, it was once the center of one of the country's larger coal mining operations. The Atchison, Topeka, and Santa Fe railroads were built through the area, attracting many looking for jobs. By the turn of century, both of my parents' families were living in Osage, drawn by the a small coal mining operation. After the mining petered out, Osage City served a small but fairly rich farming area. It was a small town in the heart of the country where the farmers would come to town on Saturday, go to the cattle auction, and do their shopping for the week. I can still see it all now: Osage City had one main street with a cross street that took you into the residential area. The streets were cobblestone and there were no traffic lights, only stop signs. No matter where you walked—down the street, into a store, anywhere—everyone knew you. In a way, Osage City was a family. All the high school kids used to gather at the drug store, and I can remember going there after school to catch up on all the news.

Then, there was the grocery store that held my future, although I did not know it at the time. Gamba Brothers was the only grocery store in Osage City in the early years. We were distantly related to that store—one of my father's sisters was married to a Gamba—and I felt a kinship with that place even though we weren't very close to her. We would go to that grocery store to get peanut butter and jelly, which we would eat with Dad's bread as a special treat. And in those days, you could buy an eight-ounce bottle of Coca Cola for a nickel. As I think about it now, that grocery was a rock—a business lesson learned just by walking inside: People always are going to eat, and what better business could there be than that?

But, of course, I would try many other things before finding my way back to the grocery store as the source for my business.

Hard work may not necessarily always be an ingredient of success, but unless the attending physician found a silver spoon in your mouth at birth, chances are that hard work will be the solid foundation for any rewards you reap in our free enterprise system. It is no guarantee of success, but hard work—coupled with a useful product, a ready market, a mission and a commitment to excellence (plus a fair share of talent and intelligence)—gives the entrepreneur a leg up.

Being born and raised in the Midwest gives one a running start in the hard work department. The Midwest work ethic really exists, and I'm convinced one of the reasons MAJERS became successful is the fact that both my parents and I were products of a small town in middle America where that work ethic flourishes.

I don't know if my upbringing is typical of today's businessman, but it provided me with a background of morality, work and study habits, frugality, self-worth, and discipline that guided business decisions later in life. All this was taught with my parents' quiet intelligence, resourcefulness, and compassion, which inspired me as I was growing up in the Midwest.

Before I could stock the shelves of the grocery, I stocked my father's bakery. Not only was he hardworking and good at what he did, he was dedicated to demanding six-day work week that was required of a baker. But he also arrived at the bakery at eleven o'clock each night, preparing bread and buns, cinnamon rolls and sweet rolls, and cakes and cookies for the townspeople who would begin their workdays six or seven hours later.

People loved my dad. He was honest and fair with everyone and the doors of his bakery were never locked—he welcomed the local police and the night owls whether it was twelve noon or twelve midnight. When Dad finished making the day's bakery goods, he would go over to his sister's café and have breakfast before going home.

He was only 5'5", but to me, Dad was a giant: a patient teacher, a churchgoing Catholic, and a believer in right and wrong. "If it is heading in the right direction or down the right path, have patience," he would tell me, "If it is wrong and you know it is wrong, do not tolerate the situation. Do something about it and correct it if you can, but do not tolerate it."

Beside Mom and Dad was my older brother, Otto Joseph Scribante, Jr. (known as Junior at home and Otto at school). Two years older than I, Junior was my role model. I tagged along with him and his pals, not always with their approval. Junior and I worked at Dad's bakery as soon as we were big enough to be a help instead of a nuisance. One of our earliest duties was to deliver rolls and bread on our bikes to the restaurants before breakfast. An especially good customer was the restaurant at the depot. Those were the days when the arrival of passenger trains in town was an important civic event.

I was given the name Adrian James Scribante after my father's brother, a cumbersome name that we shortened to Adie. Adie was short, but better than Adrian— a name I had to defend before I was, mercifully, able to change it to A.J. My parents and our teachers always called me Adrian, and I was teased because it sounds the same as the girl's name. When we were living in Chicago and I was in the fourth grade, I can recall a bully teasing me after school about being a girl. He pushed me over and I hit my head on a concrete pillar. I had been taught not to fight, but at that moment that lesson went out the door. I hauled off and punched him straight in the nose, hard enough that he didn't call me a girl anymore.

Junior and I acquired a fondness for mischief early on, but in the eyes of our mother we could do no wrong. When I was four and Junior was six, we had an apple tree in our yard and we decided it would be a great idea to throw some rotten apples at the driver of a passing car. One of the apples smashed into the windshield, making quite a mess. I don't remember which one of us scored the direct hit, but the driver stopped and chased us up the front steps of our house and onto the porch. Mother heard the commotion and came out running.

"Your boys hit my car," yelled the driver.

"My boys would never do that," she said. "Not my boys."

But the driver had seen it, he insisted.

"My boys are good boys," she continued. "I know my boys would not do that."

The driver could tell my mother believed us, and he went off, cursing. Junior and I expected punishment, but none came. Even at our young ages, the message was clear: mother trusted us completely, perhaps more than she should have. She smothered us with unconditional love, the kind that creates a strong sense of ego and that, as I would later learn, isn't such a bad thing to have when selling things to put on shelves.

■ ■ ■

In 1943, when Junior was fifteen and we were living in Monet, Missouri, he entered a high school track meet and an event occurred that would change all of our lives forever. It was raining hard so the meet was moved into the gymnasium, a place tragically unsuited for the short sprints. Ordinarily, the sprints ended with the runners buffered by mats hung on the gym walls, but this time the mats were not in place. Perhaps they were being used for the jumping events. In any case, Junior smashed against the brick wall and was knocked unconscious.

He would never regain conciousness.

I had been in school that day, and I distinctly remember the strange feeling of coming home to an empty house. Finally, someone came to get me and we rushed to the hospital. There Junior, my big, strong brother who had never shown any weakness, was laying motionless in a hospital bed. But we were told it was merely a brain concussion, and that he would soon awaken.

After a brief stay, Junior was discharged and sent home. I fed him orange juice through a flexible straw, shedding tears as I witnessed my older brother in this condition. A few days later, someone, though I cannot recall who, got me out of class to tell me the dreadful news: my brother had died. Many of the best doctors were fighting in the war, and the doctor on duty had failed to diagnose that Junior had severed an internal artery. Over a period of three days, Junior slowly bled to death in his bed.

Life forever changed in that instant. Seeing Junior in the hospital bed had been hard enough, but I never thought he wouldn't find a way to beat the accident, just as he had beaten every obstacle he'd ever faced. I was heartbroken. Junior was my brother and best friend. In a childhood marked by constant change, Junior had been my one rock, the one friend I would always have.

My father was a pragmatic man, though not without emotion. I think he accepted Junior's death as best he could and tried to move on. My mother, on the other hand, was devastated. Junior was the kind of boy who would be the apple of any parent's eye. His teachers loved him and his peers respected him. He was always the center of attention, a born leader that other kids looked up to for guidance and also turned to for fun. He was as good at football as he was at basketball and track. He played the clarinet in the school band.

The loss of a brother and a pal was great.

After the funeral I was sent off to Boy Scout Camp. My family felt that it would be a good environment for me to deal with my grief. I was able to share some camaraderie with other boys by swimming in the river, doing activities in the woods, and sitting around a bonfire at night. It helped me greatly to be around others my age when I had just lost my closest friend.

When I returned I was expected to assume the duties of my brother.

"Now that Junior is gone you're going to have to come to the bakery every morning and deliver the bread," Dad told me. "I'll pay you the same as I paid Junior—$5 per week."

I had had jobs, sure: paper routes and shoveling snow. But now my job was delivering bread—a crucial commodity—to the restaurants and the train depot. Those were the first shelves I had the responsibility of filling.

My mother never felt comfortable in Monet after Junior's death. So in 1944 my father sold the bakery and we moved back to Osage City, back to square one. He bought the same bakery he had sold nearly a dozen years before. This was a return home for my mother, the place of her family and friends of an earlier, happier day. But returning to Osage was bittersweet, for while it meant coming back to the familiarity of family and friends, it held memories of a happier time for our family when we were whole.

I had been a delivery boy at Dad's bakery in Monet, but when we moved back to Osage City after Junior's death, I became his one-man, full-fledged crew: up at 5 a.m. and at the bakery within minutes. I was fourteen years old, a freshman in high school, and a part-time baker.

Back in Osage, Dad showed enormous patience as he trained me in the bakery business, especially when he took a chance and let me decorate the birthday and wedding cakes. He considered his cakes to be his gems—"the essence of the Osage Bakery," he called them—and he trusted me to do things right. At sixteen, I was close to becoming a professional cake maker, such an expert that, many years later, when Dad sold the bakery to Al Bunger from Germany, I was hired to teach Al the art of cake decorating. Cake baking appealed to my artistic talent. I loved creating something from scratch—start to finish. This would also be good training for my later businesses.

While Dad was a patient and understanding man, he was nobody's fool. One of my after-school jobs was to prepare the bread dough so it would be ready when he arrived at the bakery each midnight. One time I forgot an important ingredient—salt—and I knew the dough wasn't going to rise but I didn't know how to fix it. I had been horsing around with Donnie, who helped clean up the bakery. I didn't want Dad to discover my lapse because I knew he expected better of me. So I buried the entire mess in a hole in the alley behind the bakery, then covered it over with gravel and made another batch.

But the dough apparently still had some oomph in it, and when the morning sun rose, the earth behind the bakery too began to rise as well, creating a small hump in the gravel pathway. It was a Saturday morning, one of the few days my father and I worked all day together, and when I arrived to help he asked me about the mess out back. He had seen the lump, had kicked it and discovered the dough, and my secret, beneath his feet.

He simply told me that if anything like that happened again to just give him a call and he would straighten it out. "A mistake won't hurt our relationship," he tried to tell me, "Talk to me." I got the message.

He could also be firm when he wanted to make a disciplinary point. Like most teenagers, I tested his rule about my evening curfew. One night I pushed too far, and he told me the next time I came home late I would find a packed bag of my clothes on the porch. "Don't bother to come in," he added.

I got that message, too.

At school, I was never the popular athlete that my brother had been, but after getting permission from my parents to compete in sports in my sophomore year, I did the best I could. I played football, was a substitute on the basketball team, became editor of the yearbook, and was a member of the student council.

At the age of seventeen, I was 5' 8" tall and weighed 145 pounds. That was not very big for center, the position I played on the high school football team. For two years I took a pounding, especially in practice, from one of our larger backs, a farm kid named Buck who outweighed me by about forty pounds.

After two years of that pounding, the coach took me aside and told me:

"Here's your chance to be our first string center this year. You've worked two years in practice and you've spent a lot time on the bench. Do you think you are ready?"

I said, "Yes!"

My father taught me, "Win as though you were accustomed to it, and lose like a gentleman." But losing has always been hard.

As one of the smaller schools we were not the best in the league, but our team won more games than we lost. At the end of the season I wore my football letter with great pride of accomplishment and much personal satisfaction for having persisted through the gruelling practices. My very best friend in high school, Chuck Ford, played quarterback and sort of took the place of my brother.

My father had played baseball as a kid, and he loved the game, visiting Omaha each year since 1958 for the College World Series. He didn't really understand the game of football, but he was always in the stands for my home games. I cherished his interest, and understood that he couldn't attend my away games because his work came first. Because of Junior's death, Mom still could not bring herself to attend any games. Even though my Mom wasn't there in person, I always knew she was proud of me.

After school and football or basketball practice, I always headed back to the bakery. Dad usually left somewhere between noon and 1 o'clock, often to play a game or two of pool before going home for a rest. My mother and my cousin, Connie, handled sales until closing time at 5:30.

I was the clean-up man. I washed pots and pans, cleaned the oven, dusted the counters, mopped the floor, set the dough for the next day, and swept up. We had a wood-burning stove that heated our oven, and it was my responsibility to chop wood and bring the right amount inside before I went home for supper, usually eaten with my mother since dad was already asleep, waiting for his eleven o'clock alarm.

Then I started my homework.

On the Friday nights our football team played out of town. I sometimes got home late, but hurried directly to the bakery. I would work with Dad from midnight to noon on Saturdays, which gave us a chance to talk. I didn't seem to suffer from this routine, nor did my grades. On the positive side, it taught me discipline and how to make the best use of my time. My father's regimen was not drill-sergeant discipline, but one that taught me how to live a well-ordered life. I'm fortunate to have learned that lesson early.

In my senior year, there was a competition to name what was called "The King of the Senior Class." The whole class voted, narrowing down a big field to two candidates on the merits of academics, personality, and achievement. I couldn't believe it when the last two standing were me and Johnny Earhart, who was an overachiever in every possible field. The final vote would be on looks alone: our photos were sent to Chi Omega Sorority at Kansas State University and the girls voted on who should be king.

Impossibly, improbably, incredibly, I won. For many it would have seemed a trivial dubious honor. But to me, it symbolized a personal transformation that I hadn't yet recognized. I had always felt like the shy kid in my older brother's shadow. I hadn't been nearly as adept as him in either social activities or sports. With Junior's death, I'd lost my best friend and role model. I spent two years warming the bench for my high school football team, and had spent most of my free time dusted in flour, helping my father support our family. But I'd also been forced to grow and forge my own identity. Now, I'd suddenly realized that along the way I had become someone that my peers respected and admired.

That year, the inscription under my yearbook photo read, "Adrian paddles his own canoe, and paddles it well."

But I would soon learn the hard way that being a high school star in Osage City, Kansas, didn't mean a thing to the outside world.

THE SHELF OF

Self-Improvement

"Have you saw Claude?"

The words were out of my mouth without even a thought that I'd mangled them, butchering the chief tool of a salesman/shelf-stockers trade: language.

Here I was, a college sophomore, a new member of Sigma Phi Epsilon fraternity, and I couldn't even speak English properly.

"Have you *saw* Claude?" I asked, looking for my friend and fraternity brother Claude Shivers. I was with my girlfriend, who pointed out that I had mistakenly said "Have you saw Claude?" instead of "Have you seen Claude?" and, surely, this must have been an innocent slip of the tongue.

But it wasn't merely a slip; it was a pattern. My father had repeatedly told me the importance of public speaking. He'd seen it first-hand at his bakery conventions, where he told me that men at the podiums were the men going places. "I want you to be able to speak on your feet," he told me. "I want you to take all of the public speaking classes that you can get."

I did as Dad insisted, taking public speaking in high school, and, amazingly, getting an A, despite the fact that I couldn't properly speak English!

"I'm going to give you an A because of your creativity, your presence, and your confidence when speaking on your feet," the teacher told me. "But, A.J., I have to tell you, you butcher the English language. Your grammar is just terrible."

Because I had always found a way to get my message across, I hadn't given it much thought—until now. I was now in a fraternity at Kansas State University and my girlfriend was looking at me like I just fell off the turnip truck.

"Have you *saw* Claude?"

That might be okay in Osage city, but it wouldn't cut it in Manhattan.

Not even in Manhattan, Kansas, home of Kansas State, where I had come to jumpstart my future. I would have to learn everything—beginning with how to speak proper English. I would have to learn manners. I would, basically, have to learn how to live in a new and different way. I had come to the right place to begin: the Sigma Phi Epsilon fraternity house. Our manners-obsessed housemother and a Kansas Emily Post, Mother Erickson (everyone called her Mother E), would be influential in acclamating me in my new environment and life.

Mother E was a great lady. She wanted to help all of the guys with ways to improve their lives through good grammar, manners, and social graces. She recognized that I needed help in this area and I quickly learned to respect her teaching. Someone always escorted her to dinner and to the social functions outside of the house, and it was an important learning experience for me. No matter how smart or talented I was, I needed to speak and behave appropriately to be respected in a professional environment.

■ ■ ■

That I even got to go to college was a miracle. We were hardly affluent—my parents had only had a limited formal education—yet both of them wanted me to attend college. So I enrolled in Kansas State University in 1947, selecting it over the other state schools because it offered a major in, believe it or not, milling chemistry (the milling of wheat into flour, which, of course, was integral to our family baking business). It seemed to be an appropriate major, and I was thankful that Dad had somehow scraped together the $800 for tuition and living costs—cake by cake, doughnut by doughnut, loaf by loaf.

My first year at Kansas State was a spartan one. The course of study was not exactly inspiring. My father drove me to campus and dropped me off. He paid the bills and I studied. I didn't own a suit and had to borrow one for the yearbook picture. I never had a date, and an occasional beer at Kites Beer Hall with the jocks who lived in quarters underneath the West Stadium was just about it for leisure activities. I was concentrating on finding my future, so while I studied milling chemistry I kept my mind open to other opportunities.

After a year, milling chemistry had become drudgery, and Dad wasn't sure he was getting his $800 worth. If this was what college was all about, I didn't like it.

So some of my buddies and I decided to do the logical thing in 1948: join the navy. I enlisted for three years and set off to see the world. The Navy was a logical choice for me; my father had been a sailor, as were his two brothers. One had retired as Chief Petty Officer after twenty-five years, while the other, my namesake, had been lost at sea. After I enlisted and completed boot camp, an officer came to me and invited me to go to officer training school. He had seen my straight "A" record in college and was impressed. But being an officer would require a six-year committment, and I wasn't ready for that. So after boot training, I was assigned to a role I knew well, and the navy sent me to baking school in New Jersey.

I served most of my naval duty as a baker aboard the USS *Askari ARL-30*. I was at the top of my class, and you can understand why. The nation was at peace when I joined up, but in the summer of 1950, President Harry Truman ordered a so-called police action when North Korean troops invaded the south. My ship became part of the amphibious force heading from San Diego to Japan. I baked bread for my ship and six other ships that didn't have bakers on board.

I spent a shift each day baking for the crew, and another shift manning a gun. During the invasion by U.S troops in Inchon Harbor, we were the only ships that could get into the beach and support the marine landing of the Inchon invasion. Our ship was in the combat zone for a year, during which time a ship next to us was attacked and lost several men. It's an anxious moment for a twenty-year-old when the enemy strikes; no one never really knows how they'll act in that situation until it comes. Fortunately we came through it unscathed and fulfilled our military mission. We evacuated the troops at Hungnam as our last duty.

We returned to San Diego where I was due to be discharged in June 1951, but President Truman extended all enlistments and I was called upon to serve a fourth year.

I served it at San Diego, once again as a baker. I needed assistants, and my superiors would assign the mavericks to me—guys with poor disciplinary records who couldn't get along with other petty officers. One guy in particular, a high school football hero, was an outlaw. The Marines had tossed him in the brig several times for which he was punished with arduous batteries of pushups, but he remained an incorrigible member of the crew. He had a more than healthy ego and was searching for ways to get recognition. Others were offended by his arrogant behavior and tried to order him around. To add to this, his work tended to be very sloppy, which would also make his superiors mad.

When they assigned him to me upon one of his returns, I sat down with him and we talked about his achievements in sports and his life at home. He was amazed that anyone really cared about who he was and where he came from. He quickly grew to respect me and did great work in the bakery.

I didn't understand the dynamics of leadership at the time, but I knew how to show respect for people. I had a way of getting people to do things others couldn't, simply by my willingness to show that interest in the lives of other human beings. When people feel valued and respected for the hard work they do, they are more apt to want to continue performing at the same high level of expectation.

Besides helping me mature and providing me with insights into my own character, the navy provided me with two other benefits: the realization that being a baker, much as it fulfilled my father's life, was not going to be my life's work; and secondly, it gave me a free education. The G.I. Bill of Rights, along with money I had saved, meant that I could return to college without worrying about finances.

Though I was now a man in years and experience, like many at that age I still had no idea what I wanted to do with my life.

■ ■ ■

Between my discharge from the navy and the time I returned to Kansas State, I had the opportunity to reflect on my lack of solid academic direction during my earlier school days. Milling chemistry! It was a crazy major leading to one direction: a life in baking. I may have been experienced at it, but baking was the last thing I wanted to do after a childhood of working for my father and a navy mission comprised of the same task.

High schools didn't have counselors then, so nobody ever sat down with me and asked, "What do you want to do with your life, A.J.? What motivates you?" I guess the only counseling I received came from my father, whose horizon was limited pretty much to the bakery business.

When I returned to Kansas State in 1952 my attitude toward a college education had entirely changed. I left the navy ready to learn and hopeful that I would find the path to the exciting and lucrative future I'd always imagined.

I bought a 1950, light green, two-door Ford with low mileage. Dad helped me pick it out and it was a beauty. The car gave me freedom and the chance to have a date without trying to borrow a car or work out a double date. It was my luxury and it put me on a par with some of my wealthier friends.

But what changed my life was not the car but the decision to pledge a fraternity, Sigma Phi Epsilon, during my second year back on the campus. I had changed my major to chemical engineering in the hopes that someday I'd make a lot of money and was able to establish myself as a good student. But by my junior year it was time to enjoy the social side of college and I finally heeded the adage, "Never let your books interfere with your education."

■ ■ ■

I didn't know a soup spoon from a tea kettle and had no idea of how to negotiate the social graces of a proper dinner table. With patience and kindness, Mother E taught me everything from how to eat (slowly, instead of in one gulp) to how to speak ("seen Claude" instead of "saw Claude"). It was a slow process, something of an informal finishing school. But when she was done with me, and the other hay-seed in our fraternity house, we were well-mannered, proper men, ready to go out and stock the shelves of our chosen occupations.

Additional guidance came from my girlfriend in the Kappa house, Martha Helmers. I met Martie, as she was known in college, at a Sunday gathering at the Sig Ep (Sigma Phi Epsilon) house in 1953 with the Kappa Kappa Gamma sorority girls. We had a few dates that semester.

Over Christmas that year I was working in Kansas City delivering mail, and she invited me for dinner at her house to meet her parents and her brother. The second semester we spent more time together going to social functions and seeing one another when I'd take her out to dinner or to the movies. We grew very fond of each other.

The summer of 1954 I took a job in Pittsburg, Kansas, working for Spencer Chemical Company, and would drive to Kansas City occassionally to see Martie and her family. We grew to love each other, and though her parents liked me in many ways, her mother was not ready to have me as a son-in-law. Martie's mother had always planned for her to marry a nice young man from Kansas City, perhaps from a well-to-do family, and my Catholic background was not something that Martie's parents wanted for their daughter. Martie and I realized this and our relationship did not grow past college. At graduation, I met her in-laws to-be.

Many years later, in 1974, Martie's husband contacted me about giving a sales presentation at Frito-Lay in Dallas. I accepted, and while there Martie and I met for a brief visit. It was great to see her again. Though our lives took different paths, Martie's influence on my social development was a benefit that has helped me throughout my life. She taught me the proper way of doing things and never seemed embarrassed by my lack of refinement.

For extra money I worked in the chemistry laboratory and waited tables at the Tri Delta sorority house. And whenever I needed extra cash for a date, a pal and I painted house numbers on curbs—one dollar for each—in Manhattan's residential districts. We could easily earn $20 in a Saturday's labors, and $20 took you a long way in those days.

I was serious about my studies, carrying eighteen to twenty-one hours a semester. I found math easy and had no trouble with my engineering courses. And even though I was a member of Sigma Tau, the honorary engineering fraternity, I was not the most enthusiastic chemical engineer Kansas State ever graduated. But there was one tremendous benefit from a major in chemical engineering: acquiring an ability to conceptualize problems. In chemistry, you cannot see what is happening, but when the solution turns from white to green you have to be able to understand what happened, to "see" it in your mind. This ability would serve me well when I began my career in stocking shelves.

By the time I was a senior I knew I was taking the wrong major, but I had already more or less wasted a year in milling chemistry before enlisting in the navy. And I sure wasn't going to waste any more time by changing to something else I might have been better suited for, like business administration or the humanities.

I remember an engineering professor told me, "You're a very dogmatic young man, A.J." I didn't know whether to smile or frown. I looked up "dogmatic" in the dictionary and saw it meant "strong-minded" and "opinionated." I thought about that. It helped me temper my approach to others. My father was a dogmatic individual as well, and while he could be firm and direct, he was still a loveable man. I was proud to be a chip off the old block.

Thanks to the love and guidance I received from my mother and, though in a different way, my father, my personal strength developed and I was blessed with things that not even Mother E could have taught me: compassion, persistence, ego, and never letting the word "no" stop me from achieving my goals. These are critical traits for anyone going into a career filling shelves.

Though I didn't know what I wanted to do, I knew I wanted wealth, a piece of the rock. I wanted to join the world of business suits, new cars, country clubs, and cross-country travel. But I had no idea how to get there with my chemical engineering degree, so I took whatever came my way figuring, as I would do in every step of my career, that a path would eventually emerge.

When graduation came, I had received three firm job offers, which was about par for engineering majors at the time: Spencer Chemical Co. in Kansas City; a water softener company in Pittsburgh; and Union Carbide, who wanted me to join its Kansas City office. Union Carbide also offered six weeks in New York City studying at the corporate training school. Because of that, I chose Union Carbide.

I left K-State with mixed emotions. I was excited about heading towards a job and glad to be done with some of the classes, but I was also sad to be leaving a special environment of good friends and relationships that I had loved. Mom and Dad came to my graduation and I could see the joy and pride they shared to have their only son earn a college degree.

My engineering days were over before they began, but the seeds that eventually would flower into the MAJERS Corporation were just being planted. I was twenty-six years old, a full-time employee for Union Carbide, and it was time to hit the road for America's major chemical manufacturing company.

I had found my first real shelf to fill.

THE SHELF OF

Failing Upwards

When I started out I was hungry. I wanted to make a lot of money, to accomplish something, and to reap the rewards of success: a nice car, a big house, and a country club where I could play golf. Most of all, I wanted the feeling of accomplishment that comes from making a contribution to society.

For a person from honest yet humble beginnings, this ambitious goal was going to be difficult to achieve. While I had enough money to live on during my final years at Kansas State, there was never much left over for frills. I had been exposed to a better life, and I wanted to be a part of it.

Each fall one of my fraternity brothers, Bob, returned from summer vacation with a new car. And not just any car, but a classy Buick convertible—the kind that turned girls' heads.

My father had taught me to be frugal: "If you can't pay for it with cash, you can't afford it," he said. Needless to say, I didn't have a new car each year.

On weekends, when I accompanied Bob or other friends to their impressive homes in Salina or Kansas City, I glimpsed a lifestyle I had only heard about. I told myself that when I got out of college I was going to do something significant.

My determination to land a job that paid well was one of the primary reasons I started with Union Carbide. It was a large company with reasonable opportunities for advancement and the money from my sales efforts would be, to a large extent, based on how hard I worked—or so I thought. The company sent me to New York for six weeks of product education and sales training. While there, I was assigned to give a report on the uses of silicon, and it was the first time that I learned the value of approaching a situation with a creative and different approach.

Silicon was reasonably new in 1957, although it could be found in many applications. Although it was not yet used for breast implants, silicon was being used in a myriad of household and industrial products. I asked myself, "How does one sell silicon?" Rather than just delivering the same, expected, and dull report, I decided the best way was to be entertaining and incorporate an engaging sales tool. I devised a caricature I called Mr. Silicon, a bright, smiling little character in the shape of a raindrop with feet, eyes, mouth, a little body, shoulders, arms, and hands. Mr. Silicon had a personality, and he kept most of my Union Carbide class members from their usual afternoon practice of nodding off.

Another good thing came out of my time in New York. At one of the sessions I met Pat Murphy, a young administrative assistant to the chairman of Union Carbide. Pat personified what I thought I wanted to be—a man who was proper, well-dressed, and had great style. I spoke to him several times, trying to work out how he had been able to progress up the corporate ladder so quickly. "Well, I started with the company in Peoria after graduating as a civil engineer," was all he told me. What he didn't tell me, and what I subsequently found out, was that he had married the boss's daughter. Since the boss had only one daughter, I'd have to climb that ladder through ingenuity and hard work.

Shortly after my training and a stint in Kansas City accompanying other salesmen on their rounds, I was given my own territory with responsibility for sales. "Omaha," said my supervisor. And I thought, "Okay, Omaha. Big city. Big opportunity. Big advancement. Big money."

But as soon as I got to Omaha, I wasn't sure if it was for me anymore. It wasn't the cleanest of cities, and as I drove over the bridge into town I could see newspapers blowing all over the street.

"What am I doing here in Omaha, Nebraska?" I said to myself.

I was there, of course, for a salary, at a level I'd never known before: $500 a month.

I was alone in a new city, but I met a lot of people quickly. One of them was the escort, in charge of all escorts at one of Omaha's biggest social events: The Aksarben (Nebraska spelled backwards) Ball.

"Why don't you come down and be an escort for one of the ladies?" he asked me.

I had no idea what he was talking about. He explained that the Aksarben had "princesses" and "countesses." Princesses were local girls from Omaha and the countesses from out state, about twenty-five of each. They needed single guys like me to serve as escorts to the various events.

So there I was, barely in town a few months, renting my first white-tie tuxedo with tails, to escort a countess from O'Neill, Nebraska, named Connie McGinley to the Aksarben Ball. We walked into the ballroom and as I looked around, I found that I was neither uncomfortable nor in the least bit intimidated, though I may have had very good reason to be. All of Omaha was in that room.

While I was there I was introduced to Peter Kiewit, founder of Kiewit Construction Company, the Swansons, who founded Swanson TV dinners, and the Skutts, who built the great Mutual of Omaha insurance company. In fact I met all of the big wheels of Omaha, and they actually called me by name. I was not just a young man with dubious prospects; I was an escort of a countess at the Aksarben Ball.

That countess, Connie McGinley, introduced me to more elements of my new city. An accomplished outdoorswoman as well as a schoolteacher, she told me about riding horses and shooting rabbits from the saddle in motion. She also drove one of the first Edsels that had rolled off the assembly line. After our first date, one thing led to another and pretty soon she was asking me to drive her to work and keep the car. "You can drive it, A.J.," she'd say.

I grew to like Omaha more than I thought I ever would.

I was in technical sales in the division that manufactured liquid oxygen and liquid nitrogen. One of the more high-profile users of these products was the space industry. Liquid hydrogen is the fuel and oxygen is the spark needed to ignite it. Steel mills use oxygen to make their blast furnaces burn more efficiently (burn hotter, faster), the welding industry needs oxygen for its torches, and hospitals keep their respiratory patients alive with oxygen.

Industrial sales is a "relationship process" with a very long sales cycle. Things happened at a glacial pace.

My territory consisted of companies like hospitals, John Deere & Co., various small welding operations, SAC (Strategic Air Command) headquarters, and Omaha Steel Works, just to name a few. I'd call on the purchasing agents and try to sell them on various Carbide Industrial products and services—at first, liquid nitrogen. But I quickly learned that stocking shelves with liquid nitrogen is not like stocking shelves with bakery items.

When I turned thirty, I felt I was ready to be married. Not long after, I met a girl that I thought was right for me. She was a young woman who was working as a receptionist for IBM. Bob Bartizal, an IBM salesman whom I met in 1958 when we were both escorts in the Aksarben Ball, introduced us. She had been a princess at the ball two years before.

Her father was president of a small branch bank in the heart of the stockyards in south Omaha. Her mother was a nurse who thought I, a salesman for Union Carbide, was a prize for her daughter, who was twenty-seven at the time. The father wasn't quite as enthused.

At the time, I had three roommates: an insurance salesman, an industrial sales representative, and a safety equipment salesmen. We all lived in a rented house. In 1959, my three roommates got married. I married near the end of my four-year tenure with Union Carbide in April 1960.

Soon after our wedding, reality hit. Our interests were very different. She was the creative, artistic type and I was the business and sports type. She didn't bond with my folks, whom she felt were not on a par with her family.

Marriage gave me a reason to renew my determination to reach my goal of financial security. But by that time, my job at Union Carbide was becoming a bore. Worse, I could see it was not my road to riches. So, seeking to fill shelves quicker and with larger rewards, I hatched a scheme I figured would make me more money, both in my job as a Union Carbide salesman and an entrepreneur on the side.

■ ■ ■

I couldn't focus on Union Carbide. The shelves were calling me, and I had an idea to fill them: ice cream. Liquid nitrogen! If the product I was selling could freeze and preserve bull semen for the cattle industry, I reasoned, it also could freeze and preserve ice cream for the food industry. In 1959 I enlisted the financial aid of a friend, Floyd Mellen, and together we built a cheap little aluminum chamber containing liquid nitrogen. Running Dixie cups of ice cream through the chamber would freeze them as hard as a brick wall in a matter of seconds. Liquid nitrogen is 470 degrees below zero, and even its vapor registers a formidable 270 degrees below.

Ice cream is an emulsion, its particles suspended. If you let it set and then refreeze it, its ingredients settle to the bottom of the cup and you have frozen milk, which nobody wants. The quicker you freeze ice cream, the better it tastes, and liquid nitrogen froze the emulsion as soon as it was poured into the containers.

What a concept. It would produce rock-hard ice cream in seconds, which meant you could turn sugar, eggs, and creams into a saleable product better, quicker, cheaper—and, better yet, you do away with all of the fancy CO_2 equipment. You could even do it in your driveway, which is exactly what I did.

We met with a local attorney named John Cleary who conducted a patent search. Our liquid nitrogen chamber and process brought a response from the Patent Office that it was an original idea, but that more evidence was needed to determine if ours was a practical application.

However, neither of us had the $10,000 to formalize the patent process. So with that, we passed on the patent and went straight to work on creating the product. First step: getting a price on the liquid nitrogen. We calculated that it would take something like thirty railroad tank cars a month to produce what we thought was enough ice cream for our market. On that basis, we did something sneaky: we had John Cleary contact my Union Carbide boss in Kansas City to inquire about the price of thirty tank loads of liquid nitrogen.

I figured I'd make a profit on ice cream and a sales commission on the liquid nitrogen. Not the smartest idea on my part, but I thought my boss would never trace the call back to me.

John Cleary made the inquiry of Union Carbide in Kansas City, thus making it appear a potential new customer was interested. Within a few days, my boss was on the telephone about the call he'd gotten from Omaha.

"We got a guy in Omaha who wants to price thirty tank cars of liquid nitrogen," he told me, as if I didn't already know. "Do you realize what a hero you could be if you make this major sale?"

Of course I couldn't tell him I had instigated the request for information about the order.

"This is a big one," the boss continued. "I'll come to Omaha and we'll make the call together."

I tried, but I couldn't persuade him not to come to Omaha. So when my boss arrived we went to see Cleary about the order. John was very calm and very professional. He wouldn't tell my boss why he wanted that amount of liquid nitrogen, and he danced around without ever making a commitment.

Later, after the call, my boss said, "He just sounds like some Irish lawyer who wants to pocket a fat broker's fee. You keep in touch with him, but don't expect too much."

I couldn't tell if he suspected anything or whether he put two and two together, so I just agreed and took him back to the airport.

Without the funds to patent our process, combined with the need to make money fast, Floyd and I abandoned the liquid nitrogen ice cream process.

Today, we would still be collecting royalties, because liquid nitrogen is the way ice cream and other food products are preserved while being shipped back and forth across the country in trailer trucks.

By 1960 my work with Union Carbide had become rote and unchallenging. I was spending my energy instead seeking ways to develop new ventures and my lack of enthusiasm was beginning to find its way to the regional office in Kansas City. That summer, my boss notified me he was coming to Omaha and wanted to meet with me.

"Can you meet me at the airport?" he asked.

"Sure," I said.

I met his plane and he suggested we get a cup of coffee. It took him about two sips to get down to business.

"I don't really feel that this business is you cup of tea, A.J.," he said.

He cut me off before I could protest. He didn't mention the ice cream caper, but, immediately, I knew that he knew.

"I don't feel that this is the business that you enjoy," he continued. "I don't think this is a business that excites you. I don't see the production here that we see from some other people and I don't think that there is a future here for you."

"So," I said. "I'm fired?"

He didn't flinch or falter.

"I'm just here to tell to you that we're going to terminate our relationship," he said.

Then, he got up from the table, without saying another word and flew back to headquarters.

■ ■ ■

I sat there, stirring my coffee, wondering what to do next.

By then, my salary had grown to maybe $650 or $700 a month, plus a car. Now, without a car, without a salary, I went home to face the music: my wife. For me, losing my job at Union Carbide was an opportunity. For her, it was an apocalypse. "What are you going to do, A.J.?" she asked me, once, twice, a dozen times.

"I don't know at this time, but I will pay the bills," I always answered.

I knew I would do something, find something. Until then, we would have to survive on her income from IBM, where as a receptionist she was making about $300 or $400 a month. Since we were only living in a small, one-bedroom apartment at that time, our expenses were not very significant. I knew that one step would lead to another, and eventually, somehow, some way, it would deliver me toward my goal.

The first step, I thought, was to get a drink. I met my buddies at the Red Lion, a little bar where we'd gotten to know the bartender. There were four of us; all salesmen, all married. One was in insurance, another in safety programs, a third in steel. For the moment, I was in nothing, but that wouldn't last long.

One of the guys ordered a whiskey sour and, desperately seeking an avenue of opportunity to arise, I watched the bartender assemble the cocktail. He pulled out a little bottle of lemon sour mix, which he poured into a canister, along with the booze.

Something about that bottle lit something in my brain.

"Can I see that?" I asked.

He handed me the bottle. Where most people would've seen nothing more than a little bottle of cocktail mix, I saw an opportunity, something to put on a shelf.

"Lemon Sour Mix."

If one bar required the stuff, I thought, all bars would.

"Where do you buy this stuff?" I asked the bartender.

He told me he got it from Lou Finacaro, the local liquor distributor, whom I had met at the Aksarben Ball when I'd served as escort when I first got to town.

I took one of the little bottles home. I checked out the ingredients and called the suppliers of these products and placed some orders. When the ingredients arrived, I took everything into our little apartment kitchen and started manufacturing my own lemon sour mix. Never one to downplay a product, I gave it what I thought would be an attractive name: Rathskeller Lemon Sour Mix.

"You're going to do *what*?" asked my wife when she got home from the job at IBM and saw me at the sink. She looked at me like I was, well … crazy.

Crazy? Yes, certainly. But I would later learn not foolish. One step did lead to another, delivering me on a doorstep I couldn't have even imagined when I stood at that sink mixing together the ingredients for the Rathskeller Lemon Sour Mix, twenty-four little bottles to the case, which I planned to sell for $700 a case.

I called Lou Finachairo.

"Lou, I've got a product that might show you a better margin than the lemon sour mix you're currently using," I said. "It's equally as good as the product that the bartender in the Red Lion showed me. Would you be willing to give this a try?"

"Sure, A.J., I'd be happy to do that," he said.

I sold him the first case for $700 and, thereafter, about two cases of Rathskeller a month. By the time I bought the bottles, put the labels on them, and made the product, I had about a third in cost. So I was able to realize a profit probably $400 or $500 per case. I was making double my Union Carbide salary for something I was cooking up at my sink!

It wasn't a fortune. I was paying our rent and essentials, but things weren't much different from the days when I got a Union Carbide check. But we had no children at the time and we never had to stop going out to dinner. So that was the way that I had an interim income.

Lemon Sour Mix was a Band Aid for my financial needs, but I knew it was by no means my future. I had seen something infinitely better, something colossal, at the place I typically go for inspiration: a grocery store.

I found my future in a Hinky Dinky grocery store. I needed to find something that was going to provide me a livelihood. I was recently married and even before I was fired I knew early on that life as a salesman at Union Carbide was not going to be my future either. So I stopped in this Hinky Dinky in Council Bluffs, Iowa, and I asked to see the store manager. "What do you sell here that is chemically compounded that would move in high volume?" I asked.

He walked me over to a shelf and showed me a display of one-gallon jugs of bleach—Clorox, I believe.

"In a week we'll go through, easily, these one hundred cases, maybe more," he said.

"How many gallons, and how many units to a case," I asked.

"Four units to a case," he told me.

"How many stores does Hinky Dinky have?"

"Forty-two," he said, "and each store re-orders bleach on a weekly basis."

A thousand light bulbs blinked on in my brain, and my mental calculator began ticking. If he sold four hundred gallons of bleach over a weekend, multiply four hundred times fifty-two weeks in the year, and that was his store alone! Counting the other forty-two Hinky-Dinky stores in the chain, plus at least twice that number of various independents operating from the United AG warehouses, plus Safeway. These totals were stunning!

I left Hinky Dinky and called someone at Safeway, with sixty stores, and United AG Groceries, with 365; and on and on, every store with bleach sales in high numbers.

Bleach involves pretty simple chemistry, consisting of about 95 percent water and 5 percent chlorine gas. Combined in the proper proportion, you produce sodium hypochlorite in liquid form (a liquid, by the way, that smells like dirty socks). So you add something else—water softener—to neutralize the offensive smell. The main thing to remember is that chlorine gas is deadly, so proper precautions are required in blending it or my budding career may have come to an abrupt halt. That meant that I couldn't make it in my kitchen sink, and that I needed to find an industrial manufacturer.

Who can I find to manufacture a liquid household bleach?

I contacted the two or three major, established chemical companies in the Omaha area and they all said, "Yes," they could produce a liquid household bleach and bottle it under my private label. But the price they quoted was always way too high. I opened up the Yellow Pages and looked up "chemical manufacturers" and stopped at Douglas Chemical Company. But they also wanted too much money, leaving my profits at pittance levels.

My fingers continued walking down the page until I came to Lorenz Chemical, which was run by two brothers, Kermit and Art. They owned a small chemical compounding company and they were willing to lower the cost to me for a price—that price being a partnership. And not just a 50-50 partnership: they wanted two-thirds.

It never occurred to me I might have had enough credit to borrow the working capital from a bank to start a business all by myself. So I saddled myself with two partners right at the beginning, and felt my cherished goal of making money slipping away from me.

We named our company the National Allied Products Company, for no real reason except it sounded impressive and had a neat acronym: NAPCO.

We named our bleach Brite*Eyes.

Like NAPCO, I came up with the name for our bleach mostly because I liked the sound of it. Most bleach brands sounded like they were compounded in the chemistry laboratory: Clorox, Hilex, Purex. I wanted something that would brighten a dull wash day for the hard-working housewife.

Brite*Eyes. I designed a smiling face on the label, one radiating delight over the prospect of making her hubby's undershorts sparkling white.

The Lorenz Brothers and I struck a deal: They would manufacture the bleach and I'd promote and sell it. We immediately went out and bought a 2,500-gallon, vinyl-lined tank, so the acidity of the bleach wouldn't ruin the tank. Most nights I'd go down and fill that tank with water, which would be an all-night job.

The chemical manufacturer we contracted to make our bleach was already was running close to capacity producing chemicals for other purposes, so sometimes Brite*Eyes had to be concocted after midnight when normal production was shut down. Many times I went to the plant late at night and stood around while our bleach was being produced. It took several hours for enough water to be piped into the 2,500 gallon tank to produce a batch, and it was my duty to turn off the water spigot, at exactly the right time.

It was also critical to ensure the water was the right temperature. Omaha's tap water, coming from the Missouri River, is icy cold in winter and tepid in summer. We cooled it in the summer by dumping in huge blocks of ice, but only a few blocks were required in autumn and spring. We had to calculate the perfect amount of ice to use so the tank wouldn't overflow when it melted.

Once the bleach was manufactured and bottled, then the fun began. I loved selling, the stocking of shelves. I thought I'd known how to sell at Union Carbide, but

I quickly discovered that had just been order taking. This was selling. This was exciting.

Where can I get my first order? I thought.

There was a grocery wholesaler in Norfolk, Nebraska, called General Wholesale. They sold to a lot of the smaller chains in the western part of the state. I called General Wholesale and was routed to the buyer, Alvin Asay. I printed up my own calling cards with the words "Scribante Chemicals" emblazoned over a drawing of a bleach bottle. Very professional, I thought. With my calling cards in my pocket, I went to see Alvin Asay. "I want to produce a private label bleach for General Wholesale," I said.

"Can you do this in truckload amounts?" he asked.

I didn't know what he meant, but didn't want to reveal my ignorance. So all I said was, "What is it that you're thinking about, Alvin?"

"Well, we probably have somewhere in the range of maybe a 1,000 cases per order," he said.

Sounded good to me! My Brite*Eyes smile had just gotten a lot bigger!

"We could do that," I said, still not knowing what the hell he—or I—was talking about.

"What is your backhaul allowance?" he asked.

Later I would learn that backhaul allowance means that trucks in to the Omaha area would come by the plant and pick up the merchandise, for which the producer would give them a freight allowance. But at the time of my meeting with Alvin Asay, I had no idea what that meant.

"I'll have to check that," I said.

Alvin Asay looked at my calling card.

"This is Scribante Chemicals?" he asked.

I said yes.

"Your name is Scribante?"

I said yes.

"Do you own this company?"

Yes, again.

"And you can't answer my question about a backhaul allowance?"

"Mr. Asay, I don't have that information but I'll get it for you," I said.

"Well, you need to be better prepared here," I said.

When he finally took a breath from reading me the riot act, he said, "Look, there's a possibility here. Come back when you know your business better."

When I came back, I knew the bleach business, inside and out. I received the order from Alvin Asay and we began producing their private label bleach at truck-load amounts.

■ ■ ■

The normal individual hears ninety-nine "yeses" to one "no" and he's devastated. But the salesman/entrepreneur hears ninety-nine "nos" and one "yes," and he's encouraged.

The thing to do, I learned, was to offer the grocer, especially the smaller grocer, a choice. "You look like a pretty good merchant," I'd tell the grocer. "You could move fifty cases of Brite*Eyes through your store. Should I put you down for fifty cases or twenty-five?"

I never asked them if they wanted to try my bleach. I approached them with confidence, gave them a choice. If the guy said, well, we'll start with fifty-five cases, and I came back a week later and he still had twenty-five cases, I'd say cheerfully, I see you're working on it. These should be gone by the end of the week. Shall I sign you up for another fifty?

Sometimes, they'd say yes, even with twenty-five cases left on the shelf.

The other thing that helped? Mentors like Ben Foley. He was old enough to be my father and he was in the advertising business at the time, although he had made his money as a successful Omaha food broker. He was semi-retired when I asked him to help me sell bleach. He knew how to get products on shelves—and how to move them off. Together we traveled around to the Omaha supermarkets and nearby small town mom-and-pop stores selling Brite*Eyes.

Within eighteen months we owned 5 percent of the Nebraska market according to a market survey by the *Omaha World-Herald*.

Attempting to broaden our reach into other states brought disappointment. The trucking industry has less regulation today, but back then its high rates made it impossible for me to compete with bleaches in Des Moines, Denver, Kansas City, and Minneapolis. Still, I found a way to transport Brite*Eyes several hundred miles out to a place called the Outlaw Store in Wyoming by giving a return load to a trucker who carried potatoes from Idaho to Sioux City. He did it for a reasonable price to avoid an empty back-haul. I never could crack the Safeway chain, but I did put my bleach into their Omaha discount store, GEM, as a first step. And Brite*Eyes went over big at the commissary at Offutt Air Force Base, home base of the Strategic Air Command. We pretty much ran Purex off the shelves there.

About a year and a half after entering the bleach market, my partners, the Lorenz brothers, and I bought another business: Amred Food Company of Omaha. Our product? Artificial flavorings: vanilla, lemon, almond, orange, maple, and black walnut. Amred's owner had been Frank Kessler, a wonderful man who was well-past retirement age. He had recently lost some distribution systems and hadn't yet located others. I felt we could do better for the product, and I convinced my partners that we should buy Amred for about $30,000. The flavoring sold fairly well despite the fact the company did little marketing.

Whereas Brite*Eyes was a high volume, low markup item, Amred's mark-up was a fantastic 67 percent. Unfortunately, it didn't move very fast. Very few products are both high volume and high gross margin. One day, I went into one of the Baker grocery stores. After checking on my bleach, I asked the owner, Abe Baker, to borrow his duster. "What for?" he asked. "Well, I wanna dust off my product." "My God, man, if it needs dusting, get it the hell out of here!" he said.

I learned there's more than one way to get a product on and off a shelf. I listened to the customer and responded accordingly. We managed to boost Amred sales by some very simple arithmetic: we cut our case count in half.

For instance: supermarket buyer was about to drop Amred from his stores because the number of cases we moved were too low. I pointed out that our flavoring competitors' products came in cases of twelve bottles, whereas Amred was packed twenty-four to the case and we had two case combinations; one case was a twenty-four-pack case of vanilla and the other was a twenty-four-pack assorted flavor case (twelve flavors).

"Your case count isn't fair to Amred," I said.

He looked me in the eye. "That's the way we run our business. We count by the number of cases moved."

I bought his logic and began packing each flavor twelve per case. Next, I visited each of his forty-two stores, checked the Amred inventory and replaced the old cases with our new twelve-pack cases. Case movement improved rapidly. Lastly, we improved the packaging with brighter labels and newer cases. The overall appearance of the product on the grocery shelf improved. Sales skyrocketed. And the buyer who was about to throw Amred out was now ordering more.

So then when I hit the road to sell Brite*Eyes bleach, I was also selling Amred flavoring. Along the way, Geroge Beaumont, a grocery broker in St. Joseph, Missouri, agreed to distribute my bleach. I soon began peddling his products as well: a cracked wheat breakfast food called Dwarfies, a vitamin, and a window cleaner called Rave.

Before he retired, Frank Kessler, Amred's owner, taught me a lesson about selling that I've never forgotten. "What is the selling price for Brite*Eyes?" he asked.

"Forty-nine cents a bottle," I said.

"And Clorox?" he asked.

"Fifty-three cents a bottle," I said.

"Oh, so your bleach isn't as good as Clorox?"

"Of course it is," I said. "All bleach is about the same, but, if anything, ours is better."

"Then why do you sell it for less?"

I said I thought I needed an incentive for the customer to buy it.

"You're wrong about that, A.J." he said. "When the customer sees your bleach and the established brands side-by-side, and yours is cheaper, chances are they will think it's cheaper because it isn't as good. Why not sell it for fifty-five cents if it's as good as your competitor's?"

I tested this theory in a town in Iowa where I had never worked before. When the grocer asked how the product compared to Clorox, I told him, "Brite*Eyes is better." He wanted to know what I would give him if he agreed to sell Brite*Eyes at fifty-five cents a bottle. I offered one free bottle for every ten he sold. I also wanted him to put a big stack of my bleach at the end of an aisle, put a sign up, and build a special display.

He did, and I repeated the process at several other Iowa stores. Brite*Eyes moved out at fifty-five cents a bottle, just as Kessler predicted it would. "Nothing has a value until you give it value," he said.

Of course, it helps to attract the customer's attention, otherwise any product will sit on the shelf waiting for the feather duster. We used a catchy label for Brite*Eyes, and pretty soon, a coordinating promotional display complete with flashing lights. The blinking eyes, plus our label's broad smile, promised to take the drudgery out of washday, and drew shoppers to our display. Every household needs a good bleach. Why shouldn't it be Brite*Eyes?

We added discounts for supermarket managers if they featured Brite*Eyes in their weekly newspaper advertisements: giving them twenty-five green stamps per bottle. We printed coupons: ten cents off per bottle. We always looked for ways to tie in with a store's other promotions. We knew that a mention in a newspaper ad, for instance, could double, triple, even quadruple weekend sales.

Newspaper ads. They were very useful tools in moving items off grocery shelves. And soon, the ads would point me toward the direction of my dreams.

■ ■ ■

The food industry is an extremely competitive environment and the stakes are high. Stamina is a must. Every week there's a new candidate for the promotional display space, the retail newspaper ad, and the weekend sales volume. But when you succeed in getting your product sold, seeing it placed in distribution and purchased by the consumer, the reward and personal satisfaction are tremendous.

You really learn the art of selling when you sell to the grocery trade. The grocery buyer deals in thousands of products, which means he deals with scores of sales people. I spent a lot of time waiting inside buyers' offices, but I also learned how to sell, how to deliver and promote a product, and how to satisfy my customer.

Trouble was, the money wasn't piling up. Certainly not enough to say I was approaching my financial goal. And after four years, it was dawning on me that I was helping provide a fairly nice living to two men who were doing very little for their share of the profits.

I pointed out to them the virtues of fair play. After all, I was the guy going out and calling on buyers, building displays, expanding the market. A one-third share for me wasn't right. I should own at least 50 percent of the company with the other 50 percent shared by the two of them.

My plea fell on deaf ears. Those two had a good thing going and they weren't about to let go. But I did persuade them to take the matter to an independent arbitrator, and let him investigate and come up with a non-binding recommendation. They agreed, and we hired an attorney by the name of Jack North. I didn't know North, but he taught law at Creighton University and had a fine reputation for fairness.

After North completed his investigation, he told me it was a lost cause.

"You're never going to change their position," North said. "You have vastly more talent than they do, but you're stuck with them. My recommendation is to pick up your shorts and get the hell out of there."

Not what I wanted to hear. I wanted somebody to put his arm around me, comfort me, and assure me a way could be found to bring me more money from the partnership.

So I went to see a second attorney, my friend Gerald Collins, who confirmed North's findings.

"One more piece of advice," he said. "When you leave, don't look back. Don't ever feel you were taken advantage of. Don't carry a grudge. Chalk it up as part of your educational process."

And that's just what I did. I sat down with the brothers one more time, but they refused to reconsider. So I told them I wanted out. They claimed they had made a sizable investment in equipment that hadn't been amortized, along with a few other hard luck stories, none of which were true. But in order to be free of the partnership as quickly and cleanly as possible, I agreed to accept a payment of less than $500 for my one-third. I did get something else: an on-the-job advanced degree in business management.

They kept Brite*Eyes and Amred, but they made little or no effort to market the products, and except for the commissary at Offutt Air Force Base where Brite*Eyes was available for years, their business gradually declined. They eventually filed bankruptcy over some environmental problems with the government. And then, National Allied Products Company, my beloved NAPCO, was no more.

I took Gerald Collins's advice. I never looked back.

I had started selling bleach with the goal of making a lot of money. True, I made enough to live comfortably, but it didn't take me long to realize such a goal wasn't going to satisfy me. I needed a mission in life rather than a goal. One is short term and selfish, the other is lifelong and would provide me with the satisfaction of helping others.

Of the many people who have helped me over the years, Gerald Collins's advise was invaluable on several occasions: one was the Bleach Company; another was with the *Omaha Magazine* I later published; and one was with the final ownership structure of MAJERS. At that time I said to Gerald, "Your legal bills are for less than the help you have given me; how can I ever repay you?" In response, he told me this story: "When I was a young lawyer I received help from a judge and when I asked him the same question, "How can I ever repay you?" he said, "If a young man ever comes to you for help and you refuse him help, then you have denied me payment." He said, "I've just paid off my debt to the judge! You will find a way to repay me as you walk your path of life."

THE SHELF OF

Finding Your Mission, No Matter How Seemingly Mundane

"The one single key to good mental health is to establish a mission in life and stick with it"—Karl Menninger

As I'd discovered, money is a hollow goal without a mission to give it life. MAJERS not only provided me with a mission, it gave my life meaning.

I started MAJERS in 1963 and it was a monumental struggle for the first five years. Like my seemingly harebrained schemes in freezing ice cream and bottling lemon sour mix, the idea of what would become MAJERS sprang from seemingly improbable roots: the grocery store ads in the daily newspaper.

In an attempt to expand my bleach "empire" beyond its limited geographic boundaries, I had subscribed to newspapers in other cities to learn what bleach was selling for in larger markets where I might sell my product: cities like Des Moines, Minneapolis, Kansas City, and Denver. The ads showed me that my competitors' prices were lower than mine, so low that I couldn't be competitive. That knowledge stopped me from expanding into these markets.

But it was more than that. Reading those newspaper ads over a period of months planted a seed in my mind.

If I wanted to know what bleach was selling for in other cities, wouldn't other manufacturers also benefit from the same information? What was Maxwell House coffee selling for in Minneapolis? Denver? Kansas City? If my product was Hills Brothers coffee, wouldn't I want to know what the supermarket was selling Maxwell House for in Des Moines? And wouldn't the same information from Memphis, Chicago, Los Angeles, or Boston be valuable as I planned my promotional campaigns in those markets?

And if coffee packagers could benefit from that knowledge, why not packagers of breakfast food, soft drinks, toilet tissue, canned beans, and the thousands of other items on supermarket shelves? The list was endless.

I knew that newspaper grocery advertisements contain a tremendous amount of information. But now I began to see that there was a way to compile such information in a handy package and make it available to major manufacturers across the country. The big players would have a keen interest in knowing what was going on with their products and their competitors' products.

It was another brainstorm, something that I instantly knew could be bigger than bleach. I subscribed to newspapers in the fifty to fifty-five largest markets and carefully clipped all the grocery ads.

■ ■ ■

It was early 1963. I needed to get my new business out of the house.

I found Ann's Answering Service through a friend who had an office in the Kiewit Plaza Building. We were having a beer in the lounge when I said I was looking for a small office space to get started. He said, "On the lower level is the best one in town."

I put down my beer and immediately went down and found Ann's Answering Service on the lower level of the Kiewit Plaza. "Ann" was a retired radio station advertising saleswoman whose real name was Margaret Croghan. Her service not only included answering phones, but renting desks to the twenty or so companies she represented, which, of course, made them seem like real businesses—to callers anyway. It was the perfect setup for a budding Omaha entrepreneur: no overhead, no employees, a full time "secretary," and the illusion that I was running real business out of a real office, not a rented desk in a glorified phone booth. Each client paid $35 per week for the service and the desk. We had a conference room and on Saturday, when no one else was around, I would take sixty or so newspapers from the top fifty newspaper markets and start clipping the pertinent grocery ads.

I would tag each retail grocery ad with a pre-printed sticker that showed the ACV for the retail grocery ad in each market. The tag would indicate what's known as the "all commodity volume," or what percent of the market the grocery company represented in that particular city. This approach showed the reader the potential sales volume of each retail grocery account in the various markets.

Pepsi could see that a "special feature" with VON's in Los Angeles doing 15 percent of the ACV would sell more units than a "special feature" with Safeway doing only 10 percent of the Los Angeles ACV.

I'd then take the tagged and bundled ads to Barnhart Press to be printed for a Tuesday mailing. The ads were bound together in a neat booklet measuring eight by eleven inches, easy to read, handle, and store. The cover featured one ad reproduced with the unweildy title, *Weekly Composite Market Survey—Major Market Retail Ads of Supermarket Groups Doing the Major Share of Retail Food Volume Within a Given Area.* The books placed in pre-addressed envelopes, then in bulk mailing postal bags and taken to the dock at the post office.

Some people thought I was missing a few gears; others, including my wife, thought I needed a real job with a stable salary. "You're doing what?" she sighed. What I was trying to do, what I just knew could be a success, wasn't easily explained, much less understood by someone who wasn't in the grocery business.

My first book contained one hundred pages. Ads were identified by city and by the all commodity volume each ad represented in that city. For example: Maxwell House was selling for 69 cents a pound can in Jacksonville, Florida; Krogers coffee was 39 cents with a coupon in Indianapolis; Hills Brothers was two pounds for $1.29 in Newark; and the A&P store in Knoxville, Tennessee, was giving away a free pound of its private label coffee. Our market survey would give manufacturers, for instance, Maxwell House, a simple source of information to study, extract, and then act on getting a bigger share of the market—now that they knew the price of their competitors' products and their activity in the market.

When I went to pick up the first batch of bundled newspaper advertisement at the printer, to whom I owned a sizable debt, he shot me a look that said, "I sure hope this works, A.J." I knew he was really thinking: What could be crazier than reprinting newspaper ads? Why would anyone in Seattle want to know what something is selling for in Boston? But when the printer gave me the last bag, all he said was, "Good luck!"

■ ■ ■

In February 1963 I mailed the five hundred books to retail grocery chains, wholesalers, manufacturers, newspapers, advertising agencies, and trade magazines. Each copy included an introductory letter from me and a reply card for them.

From the letter:

What is it?

The only up-to-date digest of over one hundred-fifty chain and supermarket ads run in fifty-eight cities in the U.S. every week. These stores are the ones doing the major share of the retail food business.

Full-size weekly newspaper ads are reduced photographically and reproduced in convenient booklet form.

Who uses the COMPOSITE MARKET SURVEY?

Manufacturers... Advertising Agencies... Supermarket Operators... Newspapers...

What Will the COMPOSITE MARKET SURVEY DO FOR YOU?

Tell you exactly what leading retailers are featuring in their advertising

Give you the facts—about prices being offered

Give you up-to-the minute knowledge of special deals and offers—competition.

Keep you informed on new products—test markets, features, etc.

Enable you to see cooperative advertising activities—yours and your competitors'.

I suggested a subscription from of $3.37 a week for a single copy. The annual subscription price was $175 for fifty-two weekly booklets. The economics looked good: the books cost a buck to print apiece, mailing and envelope was forty cents, making the total cost $1.40. That left a $2.00 profit per book for me.

When I got back from mailing the first batch, I returned to my rented desk and telephone at Ann's Answering Service, and I waited. And waited. And waited some more. Finally, the phone rang.

I might have answered, "Weekly Composite Market Survey . . ." or I might have just said, "Hello." But I'll never forget what the voice on the other line said. His name was Dr. Black and he said he was the research director of the Florida Citrus Commission in Lakeland, Florida.

"We'd like to place an order," he said.

He didn't just want one book, but an annual subscription. When I hung up the phone, I was ecstatic. A few days later, I opened my post office box, and there it was, my first check, $175, along with a note. "A great service—one that fills a great need." The next day, the mailbox had more annual subscriptions: the Campbell Soup Company in Camden, N.J., 26 Safeway divisions, all of the divisions of Foodfair out of Philadelphia, the Great A&P Tea Company, Kroger, General Foods followed soon after, ten subcriptions from Procter and Gamble, and two from General Foods. At the end of the first three weeks, I had sixty orders!

The sixty subscriptions so bolstered my confidence that I printed and mailed 440 solicitation samples, and more subscriptions followed. In my first month in bsuiness, I brought in $10,500, which, less my costs of $2,800, left a profit of $7,700.

By the end of the first year, I had 250 subscribers, including most all of the major consumer packaged goods manufacturers, the major retailers, several newspapers from around the U.S., and most of the major advertising agencies.

Around this time, I was having dinner with my cousin, chief surgeon at Sloan-Ketting Hospital, in New York city. As I told him about my new business, he suggested I meet a friend of his at the Murphy Co. who were the "factors" for Field Crest Mills, which provided big stores like Marshall Fields in Chicago with "inventory credit."

I did as my cousin suggested. One of the accountants at Murphy Co. had a suggestion: "When you go back to Omaha, just simply ask your bookkeeper or accoutant to check out 'Section X' in the General Accounting Procedures Manual. Don't tell them someone in New York told you that. Just ask them to review it and explain if it applies to your company."

I did and it worked. The cash flow didn't change but the bottom line did.

■ ■ ■

As my subscriber numbers grew, I developed a routine.

I'd enter the new customer addresses into a label machine, print the mailing labels for the weekly mailing, stick the labels to the envelopes then go to the printers and after 4 p.m. on Monday, when the books were printed. I'd put the books in envelopes sorted by postal zone. Then, I'd bag them and haul them to the post office dock.

I got hoarse from answering the phone, *Weekly Composite Market Survey—Major Market Retail Ads of Supermarket Groups Doing the Major Share of Retail Food Volume within a Given Area.*

I needed a short, easy-to-remember name.

I began looking through the dictionary, on billboards, and in business magazines. Finally, I went with the obvious. Since we were representing the MAJOR grocery markets in the United States, I took the word MAJOR and changed the "O" to an "E" to represent my nickname, Ed, at the time. Then I added the "S" for my last name, Scribante. I liked what I saw—MAJERS!

"It's got a strong ring to it," said the first friend I shared it with.

I hired an advertising agency to create the MAJERS's logo, and he the art director told me that I needed something strong. "When you are small and unknown you need to shout to your customers!" he said. He looked at a few of the prototypes I'd created. "Right now you are whispering, and that will never get you any attention." We talked a bit about the company and he asked, "What type style do you like?"

I saw it before I said it: the big, block, defiant letters of IBM. We went with IBM as a concept and made our logo read simply MAJERS. On the letterhead it was ¾" high in dark hunter green on light beige paper. It was perfect. Whenever a client received our letter or someone walked into their offices, they knew that MAJERS was there.

I also increased the subscription price from $175 a year to $125 for six months.

■ ■ ■

As I worked to grow my MAJERS concept, I pursued several separate ventures simultenously. I had no choice about this: MAJERS wasn't making any money, and I needed to find ways to keep body and soul together while giving my new business time to grow. As an inveterate problem-solver, there were few ideas I came upon that I didn't think I could market or improve. Further, multi-tasking came naturally to my entrepreneurial spirit. Perhaps I learned this working in my father's bakery.

I began to look upon every event in my life as a potential opportunity. It's a funny thing: when you start looking at life that way, there is no limit to the opportunities that will present themselves. Most of the opportunities that arose for me shared a common theme: they were things you could buy in a grocery store, which, of course, is where I was spending much of my time.

In those days in the 1960s, my wife, as well as most of the women in Omaha and across America, was a major consumer of hair spray, specifically Aqua Net. I tried to buy her a can in a supermarket, but was told, "Sorry. We don't carry Aqua Net. No supermarket does. You have to buy it from a beauty shop. I looked across the endless aisles. All I saw were women.

It struck me that there could be no better place for selling Aqua Net. I found the company's address of the largest beauty supplier in the area.

I set up a meeting with the owner and proceeded to tell him how I could help him increase the sale of Aqua Net significantly.

He said, "Why don't you go to work for me on a part-time basis and learn this business?" He said he'd pay me $2,000 a month for three months. Then he wanted us to meet and discuss how the company could do better. It was already successful.

I trained with his two top sales people, going from shop to shop from morning to evening.

This was truly a cottage industry, made up of mostly women who wanted to make some extra money while helping other women look pretty. We sold hair conditioners, shampoos, hair spray, eye makeup, combs, and many other beauty products to shops. The places ranged anywhere from someone's back porch, to spare rooms, to facilities with several chairs in larger cities.

After three months of working two days a week, the owner and I met again. That is when I told him, "You sell one truck load of Aqua Net, case-by-case, every three months. I could sell two truck loads a week in just the Omaha stores if you give me the okay and pay me a commission." He said no, because he would lose his "shop" business. Shops sold Aqua Net for $3.50 per can, and retail chains would sell it for $0.99. I told him if he didn't sell it in grocery stores, someone else would.

Three months later, you could buy Aqua Net in the grocery store at $0.99 per can. Customers had never seemed to complain about the $3.50 price when they could only get it in the shops, but when it hit grocery shelves across the country, the volume of sales increased nearly one-hundred fold. The shops had built the demand and the retail chains captured the volume.

Still needing some way to keep body, soul, and family together, and all I had to do is look where I always looked: on the shelves of the local supermarket. There was a salad dressing called Dorothy Lynch Salad Dressing, which I brought into the market. I put together a contract with Mac Hull, and I had 10 percent of his revenue.

I first met Mac when Ben Foley and I set up the advertising office for Ayres in Omaha. We got Dorothy Lynch just as it was starting as our client for advertising. It was very small at that time and newspaper ads served to introduce the product.

Mac was an attorney by education and the son-in-law of one of the Behlen brothers in Columbus, Nebraska. Dorothy Lynch salad dressing started in a restaurant in the area and Mac bought the national franchise from the Lynch family. He told me, "I'm not a marketer or salesperson. I plan to spend my time building the plant to produce the product and then I will be the truck driver to deliver the product. This way I will get to know the distribution centers and their warehouse people."

Mac was a hard worker and a very fair-minded guy. We worked well together. I recall sampling his product in St. Joseph at one of the Beaty Supermarkets. Carolea Beaumont and their three daughters were the "samplers." With a little lettuce and small bit of dressing and we had a new customer for the product.

As his contracted sales agent, my job was to get him distribution through the grocery chains and wholesale operations. My first step was to set up the food broker, Joe Kenney and Company, to represent Dorothy Lynch in the eastern Nebraska area. Next, I went beyond that area into St. Joseph, Missouri, and sold Beaty wholesale with the help of the local food broker. I continued introducing the product in Kansas City, Des Moines, and Sioux City until the end of the third year. By then the contract was paying $24,000.

Ben and I then signed up the Geisler Pet Products Company as an advertising client. Geisler products were sold nationally but sparsely. Their products were bird seed, hamster feed, and other associated items. It was certainly a different business.

"How do you get the customer, the birds, to eat more seed?" I kept asking. You don't. You just get more birds. Since more and more birds are imported from around the world, and since the seed was sold to pet shops, the market for bird seed was constantly growing.

Although it paid only $250 a month, the rep job allowed me to travel around the country three or four times a year visiting food conventions as the Geisler representative. My boss at Geisler agreed I would man the company booth and, at the same time, sound out potential customers for MAJERS. When I got to New York, I said, "I'd like to stay an extra day or two and pay for my own hotel room." They said that was fine, and they'd still pay my way home, and so I was left with a few days to drum up opportunities in New York.

Always looking for new opportunities, I found Old Southern Barbecue Sauce out of Kansas City, which paid me $250 a month to rep their product to the Nebraska market. The owner was Bruce Phipps. Ben Foley, the top food broker in Omaha, whom I had met when he helped me market Brite*Eyes bleach, introduced me to Bruce. He once represented Old Southern Barbeque Sauce. I represented his products as I would call on the various retail clients and outlets. "If you like barbeque, then Old Southern is the greatest," I'd tell everyone I met. "It has a very special taste and is quite appealing to the palate."

My relationship with Old Southern would be temporary, but I found a friend for life in Ben Foley, who would have a dramatic influence on my business career.

■ ■ ■

I had piecemealed a respectable income repping supermarket products: Geisler, Old Southern Barbecure Sauce, and Dorothy Lynch Salad Dressing. My contractual arrangement with Dorothy Lynch gave me 10 percent of all sales that I developed. The first year was zero; my fourth year paid me $24,000. I didn't make a lot of money from any of my sidelines, but the total was enough to live on while developing MAJERS into a full-time operation.

Once again, Ben Foley had a major influence on me. He'd first heard my concept for MAJERS almost as soon as I dreamed it up. It was 1963, and I had just sold my share in the bleach business to my partners and was in the process of putting together the "grocery ad book." Ben and his wife had gone on a three-month travel vacation. When they returned, I was already in the publishing business with a few subscribers to my new venture, MAJERS. When he heard about MAJERS, Ben instnatly said, "This is a winner and I'd like to be a part of it."

He had been such a help in advising me how to market bleach and would now become my partner in the MAJERS operation. He put up $5,000 for a half interest, and we kept his money in reserve for emergencies only. The main purpose of his investment, in other words, was to provide MAJERS with a $5,000 line of credit. He also pitched in to help with the rather tedious job of going through fifty or more newspapers a week and clipping and pasting grocery ads.

Ben was an orphan and he and his wife never had children. I think I was his "adopted son." He was a very successful food broker and made a significant amount of money. He was a very frugal man, and when he sold his brokerage business he became a real estate owner of several buildings which he rented. He was certainly financially secure.

Ben had a big heart, a great sense of humor, was fun to work with, and a very dear man. Though twenty-five years my senior, we worked and got along very well together.

When Ben retired from the brokerage, the local/national advertising agency, Bozell and Jacobs, pursued and lured Ben because of his knowledge in food marketing and sales. B & J, as they were known in Omaha, was the agency for Boys Town and the creators of the slogan, "He ain't heavy father, he's my brother."

When I ran some ads for my bleach, Brite*Eyes, I did it through B & J. That is when Ben and I met. Later, when Ayres Advertising was looking to open an Omaha office they contacted Ben. He had developed a respected reputation during his time as a food broker.

Ben asked me to join him in this advertising business, and we opened the office on the twelfth floor of the Kiewit Plaza building. MAJERS kept its desk with Ann's answering service on the lower level. It was a fun and exciting time. I knew MAJERS would eventually provide a good livelihood for me. I also enjoyed the advertising business, though it was often challenging.

We hired a secretary and all of the creative work came from the main office in Lincoln, Nebraska. We were the sales arm and client service part of the agency for consumer products.

We had Dorothy Lynch, Geisler, Old Southern Barbeque, and a Chevrolet dealer as our first customers. Ben was the "gray-haired," experienced executive-type. I was the energetic "young buck," eager to do all the legwork.

We did a good job for the Ayres Advertising Agency, but then the owner hired an advertising executive from San Francisco, a man who had worked for a top national agency, Foote, Cone and Belding. He saw the grocery ad book and was very impressed and told me he wanted to be a part of it. He offered to buy into the business. By this time, I learned how partnerships worked. With a percent, no matter how small, he could control my business. Since he and I were not brothers, I didn't want any part in that. He pursued me for several weeks but I never gave in.

This fellow did not like the idea of Ben and I doing our separate MAJERS thing on the side, so we left. He told us that our side line was too much of a conflict of interest. We agreed to leave and we took the sales accounts with us. Any advertising that would be done would still be done with Ayres, but the sales representation was ours.

When we left the ad agency I kept several of my accounts, including Dorothy Lynch salad dressing, made in Columbus, Nebraska; Geisler Pet Products Co., of Omaha; Bruce Phipps Old Southern Barbeque of Kansas City; and an Omaha Chevrolet dealership.

■ ■ ■

Some time in 1964, an opportunity came as opportunties usually do: in tandem with something else. I was having my MAJERS booklets of grocery store ads printed at Omaha's Barnhart Press. One day, the onwer, Jack Barnhart, asked me if I was seeking new investment opportunities. I never say never, so I said, even though I wasn't exactly flush with cash, "Sure, Jack"

"Well, I've got a guy who owes me a heck of a lot of money," he said.

"What does he do?" I asked.

"He publishes *This Week in Omaha*."

I knew the publication, if you could call it that. It was actually a guide to the city, a skinny what-to-do-and-where-to-go booklet, that, I immediately thought, could be much more. Jack told me that I could probably buy the magazine for its back-printing debt, which amounted to $6,500.

I went out and bought a copy. It was obvious that the owner hadn't been pay-ing much attention to his magazine. I saw where I could increase the size of the magazine from 5 by 7 to 8 by 10, creating much more room for ads and editorial. By my calculations, I felt I could make $500 a month for the magazine, once I paid off the $6,500 in debt.

I asked Jack Barnhart to introduce me to the owner.

His name was Manny Weinman and when he met me at Barnhart Press he immediately said, "So you want to be in the publishing business, Jack tells me."

"Manny, if I were willing to assume your debt with Jack, would you agree to sign over the ownership of the magazine to me?" I asked.

He looked at me like I was a life raft.

"You bet I would," he said. "I'll draw up the papers and you can come to the house tomorrow and have dinner and we'll sign them. I'll tell you things you should know about the workings of the publication and the advertisers."

The next night, over dinner and contracts, he gave me some advice about pub-lishing.

"You need to keep these clients current on their payment to you," he said. "Because they have a tendency to be slow to pay."

We shook hands. I had just become editor and publisher of my own magazine.

Manny ran the operation out of his home. He showed me the art boards with the pages outlined and the space for each week's editorial. "Here is a list of the artists I use for the ads and the name and number of my writer, Buddy Dundee," he said. "Buddy's a good talent and can help you with the book's editorial. Let's call him tonight, and I'll introduce you two tomorrow."

After introducing me to Bud, Manny took me to several of the advertisers and introduced me as the new owner. I received their support and together we were off and running. Bud was a take-charge kind of writer/editor and I was happy with that since I had other mountains to climb. He layed out his editorial plans for the next four issues. Only about 20 percent of the stories and the ads he envisions were changed by me.

Next, I met with the magazine's freelance artist. "I want this rag to take on a very professional look and some of these ads need to be redone," I said. "Talk to these advertisers and get their approval to dress up the ad and give them a price that is 50 percent greater than what you will charge me."

Within a couple of months, the magazine took on a much-improved and more inviting appearance. We expanded the size and began looking for ways to enhance the covers. The racetrack or the Ak-sar-ben Ball provided some great shots. The zoo was also a great source for cover photos, as well as baseball's College World Series.

During my first summer as a publisher, I was invited to join the other media "moguls" and fly to Lake Okoboji in Iowa for a publicity weekend. The owner of the hotel provided the plane, a DC-4. The group of twenty consisted of three television stations, two newspapers, three main radio stations, and *This Week in Omaha*. There is nothing like being part of the media when people are willing to wine and dine you for some publicity!

I found the keys to successful publications to be good editorial articles and good circulation to attract advertisers. In six months, the debt was paid and my take from the magazine was $600 per month—$100 more than my estimate!—plus all of the perks and benefits.

But something was missing. The magazine was devoted to entertainment, cultural events, sports, and the arts. But *This Week in Omaha* sounded like an insert or a giveway. I wanted the magazine to sound bigger than it was, so it could grow into an identity. So I changed its name: *Omaha Magazine*. Meanwhile, issue after issue, I continued to broadened its scope, adopt an even larger paper size, dressing it up with better photography and articles and taking advantage of those extras that fall the way of the editor/writer/publisher, including a ski trip to Vail, Colorado. Besides complimentary lift tickets, meals, and drinks—all because I was the writer of the story—I was able to write off my other expenses as publisher.

It was a very sweet sideline.

During my time as publisher, we covered a variety of different stories on a wide range of subjects. A few included: the Vail, Colorado, ski area, a stage production of Baby Doe, the Peony Park Amusement Center, the SAC Air Command, and of course, Nebraska football.

But the magazine wasn't all perks One of my first hires stole several hundred dollars, cashing for himself checks made out to *Omaha Magazine*. I'd hired him to sell and service the accounts. He called on the current advertisers and solicited new clients as well as collected some of the past due accounts. What I didn't know was that the checks from the advertisers were going into his pocket. He'd cashed three checks to *Omaha Magazine* at three different banks. He evidently had been cashing these checks for the past month or so when I got a call from one restaurant owner that I knew very well. He said, "Your guy was just in and asked if I could pay my account. We were not overdue so I told him to come back in a month. He said he would be out of town then and would like to have me pay him now. I told him that I didn't pay my bills in advance. That's why I am calling you! It just didn't strike me right."

I thanked him and called the sales guy to come to the office. He hold me the checks he cashed so I wouldn't have him arrested. I then fired him on the spot. I called the bank where we did business and they informed me that their insurance would cover the loss. Two of the three banks did the same.

When I approached the vice president of First National Bank of Omaha, he said, "We have a policy that does not allow me to cover such a happening." He wouldn't cover the money from the checks, and I always remembered that, even years later when representatives from his bank would come looking for business.

I told the vice president I would never do business with his bank again. I don't think he was impressed because *Omaha Magazine* wasn't a very big account. But MAJERS became a rather sizable one, and it never did a dollar's worth of business at that bank, not even when we were recording $35 million in annual sales.

From then on, I was more watchful in my selection of employees. I tried to find more people like Ben Foley. The start-up work we did at the beginning, with our sleeves rolled up to the elbows wasn't very inspirational to a man as smart as Ben, but he believed we had a good product and was faithful to our mission.

I owned the magazine for five years, growing it from a circulation of 2,000 per week to 6,000 per week. The advertising rate went from $350 for a full page ad to $500 per month. Our profits doubled. It was a great ride, but I was glad when it was over. I sold it to a budding artist for around $10,000.

It was time to move onward and upwards with MAJERS.

■ ■ ■

For someone whose goal had been to make a lot of money, it took a strong belief in our mission to sustain me through the hard times and long hours away from my family.

I was everything at MAJERS: janitor, payroll clerk, operations manager, salesman, and jack-of-all-trades. In the first two years I made a very small profit on sales of $100,000 and $200,000, respectively. The next year, I started my "information development" segment, which just about bankrupted me. It involved developing a computer database of newspaper special features, by brand, category, market, and advertising retailer... by both day and week. The costs were considerable, and I was running out of cash. There was no place to turn for income, so I just stopped paying bills, especially the biggest one: my printer's. Because he trusted me, the printer didn't lean on me for the debt, not until I got to the $40,000 account payable level.

"Let's go to lunch," he said one day when I stopped by to pick up an order.

He asked me to sign a loan to pay back the $40,000 over three years. The payments would be low the first year, higher the second, and highest when the balance came due on the third year. He said he would waive interest charges, as soon as I gave him his final check.

He believed in me, and I wouldn't be here today if he hadn't. As MAJERS grew, that printer handled everything, and his business grew alongside mine.

The weekly publication of national newspaper ads remained a part of MAJERS' arsenal of information to its clients even after we sold the company. Its content remained unsophisticated but extremely valuable, and it is still publshed on a weekly basis, much the way it was the very first time, proving that a good idea that fills a need has no expiration date.

■ ■ ■

After my first year in business, my partner Ben Foley, who was getting along in years, decided to make his permanent home in California. We quickly agreed that he would sell out. I asked two favors. First, because I couldn't afford to buy him out, I wanted him to sell his share to someone with whom I felt comfortable. Secondly, I wanted to be the majority stockholder. Ben and I had been 50-50, but he agreed that I should own 51 percent, and he would sell 49 percent for $5,000.

We found a buyer, Bill Wurgler, a former infantry colonel who had returned from World War II to establish his own photography and engraving shop. Wurgler was already doing the photo-engraving for the MAJERS booklet, and he knew about the business. He was also willing to pay Ben $5,000 for a 49 percent interest in MAJERS.

Bill Wurgler didn't care about sharing control with me. He had faith that some-day MAJERS would be a financial success and he was happy to have a share in it. Bill was an energetic, hard-working, easygoing fellow who was making a good living out of what had started as a one-man show. He was full of ideas, cheerful and optimistic. Best of all, he had a vacant space upstairs in his modest two-story building in downtown Omaha, and he said I could move both *Omaha Magazine* and MAJERS there, into a real office.

By this time, mid-1964, I still had my other reliable income enterprises while I was sinking or swimming with just the two ventures. But it was mostly sink with MAJERS and swim with *Omaha Magazine*.

■ ■ ■

Warren Buffett and I met at a mutual friend's birthday party. Our friend, Bob Muchemore, was the legal counsel for Mutual of Omaha Insurance Company. I recall asking Warren what his business was and he replied, "I've started an investment partnership and if you have some funds to invest I'd be happy to include you." Well at that time I didn't have any extra funds—what an opportunity lost. That was around the time of 1965 and his shares were a great buy. He wanted to know what I did and since my source documents were the local newspapers—he owned stock in the *Washington Post*—he was interested to learn more about my business.

Later on my neighbor, John Cleary, would invite Warren to his "Bluegrass Music" gatherings, which I also attended, so our paths crossed from time to time. He knew of our progress because of the many newspaper articles that were written about the tremendous growth and development of MAJERS Corporation. I met with Warren to invite him to be a speaker at one of the MAJERS national events and he was interested in our growth, but could not make the event. Then his son called me to ask if I would support him financially for his run for the open county commissioner's seat. I did that and he did win. Omaha is a small community and even if you don't spend a lot of time together, you have mutual friends and the community knows who you are. I hired one of Warren's high school chums to work at MAJERS for a short while and he told me of their friendship at one of the local meetings.

■ ■ ■

Around 1967, at the beginning of our computerized information stage, we reported to our clients the number of newspaper features and each ad's individual lineage by brand and by retailer within each market. Lineage is an advertising term that relates to the line of print in each one column inch of newspaper space. There are fourteen lines per column inch. I thought it was a pretty good system of helping clients discern how much retail grocery newspaper advertising their competitors were doing—and how much they needed to do—until the brand manager at General Foods, in the Birds-Eye Division, burst my bubble and eventually pushed me into a new dimension of service.

"This data doesn't tell me anything important," he said. "Ten ads with 100 lines versus one ad with 40 lines, what does that mean? Which is better for me?"

When I tried to explain, he waved his hands in the air.

"Why don't you come up with a method that would *qualify* the grocery newspaper features, something like best, good, fair," he said. "That way, I'd know where to spend my trade promotion dollars."

Listen to your clients, I thought on the way back to my office.

From that point on, I'd ask retailers the same question: "When you put your weekly ads together, what is your criteria?" I was told that they basically have three levels of feature ads: the "best buys," for items that carry the biggest ads and the biggest discounts to entice customers into stores to buy their grocery needs for the week. Next come lesser value features, and, lastly, products are listed at shelf price to collect the co-op advertising monies from the manufacturer.

Back at my desk one day, I had something of an epiphany.

I had been looking at supermarket advertising strictly as a business. Now, I realized that supermarkets have a soul. They're not merely shelves of lifeless objects, but a bazaar of our most precious commodities, food, and staples that we need to live. The prices of these items fluctuate with specials, coupons, and in-store discounts as much as a foreign bazaar fluctuates with bargaining. How are these staples sold? By weekly retail grocery newspaper ads and in-store displays. The first step in my company's growth was helping manufacturers learn what products were selling for in various markets. Now I could see the next step: helping them take *action* to propel explosive movement of products in supermarkets coast-to-coast.

How? The answer was as simple as A, B, C.

Instead of tracking the importance of the product features in retail grocery newspaper ads merely by size (lineage), I developed a promotional index of measuring ads by "weight," or, as we called it, the A, B, or C feature ad. After much research, I determined that what we'd call an A feature, for products given the most dominant newspaper promotion space, coupled with perhaps an in-store display and priced 25 percent below shelf price, could move product at an astronomical rate. An A ad could move ketchup six to eight times normal volume, bathroom tissue at four to five times the normal, and in other categories as much as *forty* times the normal volume. B features, for products with less newspaper ad dominance and priced around 10 to 15 percent below shelf price, also had impressive rises in sales. C features, for products with much smaller ad space and usually no discount, slightly increased sales movement by the ad alone.

I assigned value to each feature: a 6 for an A, 3 for a B, and 1 for a C. Then, we created a promotional index that studied the ACV (All Commodity Volume) size of a standard metropolitan city and the AVC market share a retail grocer commanded against their competitors in specific city areas. With this information, the manufacturer could estimate which store and what city they needed to maximize the movement of their product—and then select an A, B, or C feature to get their product moving. We called it the MAJERS Weighted Ad System, the measurement for manufacturers to predetermine and then influence their Nielsen share of the market for various products.

Suddenly, a manufacturer could make intelligent decisions on retail grocery newspaper advertising and in-store displays, as well as know where to promote their products in different markets to maximize movement, and, also, profits.

After compiling and formatting this information, I took it to the various manufacturers, and, well, you can guess their reaction. It was like giving them a rifle and a target, where, before, they had merely been shooting bullets into space. Suddenly, they could make calculated and intelligent decisions on where to market and ship their products. The MAJERS Weighted Ad System showed them *how* to move product. The other information services we provided showed them *where* the opportunities were to get the A features and to move product. What began moving most were our services. The Weighted Ad System had propelled MAJERS into another league.

■ ■ ■

Around this same time, I was invited to the A.C. Nielsen headquarters in Chicago to have lunch with the company's founder, Arthur C. "Art" Nielsen, Sr., one of the founders of the modern marketing research industry. He founded A.C. Nielsen, the world's leading marketing information company, in 1923. I arrived at the offices and was escorted to the executive lunchroom. I'll never forget the table: The long and rounded at both ends with room for between fourteen and sixteen people. I sat at Art's right and immediately he introduced me to his executive staff, by name and title, one by one, while telling me how long each person had been with the company, where they started and what position they held then.

Art, Sr. was very gracious and was very interested in what I was doing. He knew about MAJERS because the A.C. Nielsen Company subscribed to the Grocery Ad Book and had learned that we were computerizing the information.

After some brief conversation, he said he wanted to give me some valuable advice that, he said, might come in handy as I continued to build MAJERS.

"Keep in mind that your clients will have vastly more money than you will ever have, so work on their money, don't go to the bank to borrow working capital," he said. "Put a contract together. We will give you a copy of ours as a guideline, and in the contract state that you will bill 40 percent at the signing of the contract, then 40 percent after five months of work, and the final 20 percent at the completion of the first year."

He added that I should put an evergreen cancellation clause in the contract for a six-month renewal notice. "This way you will be able to protect yourself from a planning point of view and also protect your bottom line performance," he said.

He added that if I ever wanted to work for A.C. Nielsen, his door would be open.

■ ■ ■

In 1968 I was beginning to sell additional clients from our common database. The benefit was that there were no additional data collections or database development costs. Profit started to develop as a result of our syndicated product category database.

Some of the clients we gained at this time were Scott Paper, Northern Paper, Kimberly Clark, Crown Zellerbach Paper, Maxwell House, Hill Bros., Starkist Tuna, and Chicken of the Sea. Hunts Foods put me in the ketchup, tomato sauce, and tomato juice business. Later that year I landed H.J. Heinz on ketchup, pickles, and tomato sauce.

MAJERS had crossed the line to profitability. This happened as a result of increased sales, a reduction in computer costs, and the standardization of our report formats. When we installed the computers, it would cost us less than we were paying for contract midnight shift time on an hourly basis.

Red was one happy guy. He said, "Just think we have a capacity now to triple this business without significant computer cost increases."

By then, we had what every business needs: a mission statement. Ours was simple: "To help our clients better manage their promotional expenditures through the use of our information systems of the weekly newspaper advertising specials by grocery retailers."

Later we reworked our mission statement to read:

"Our mission is to be the BEST at providing information which will help our clients manage their marketing expenditures for competitive advantage."

Our slogan was: "Making our BEST work for you."

Not that a mission is all you need. MAJERS was in business for at least ten years before the company really took off and became a leading player in the field of marketing information

I knew that MAJERS was a brand new kind of business. There was nothing exactly like it in the United States. When company executives received our product and letter in the mail, we received their orders and checks and compliments. They all said they had never seen anything quite like the booklet before. It meant they were being served in a wholly new way. Subscriptions gave us the cash flow that later funded our computerized information service, which ensured our future growth—if the computerization costs didn't kill us first.

■ ■ ■

"When will you be in Cincinnati next?"

It was 1966 and the brand manager at Procter & Gamble said he had something important to discuss with me. P&G was subscribing to seventeen copies of the grocery ad book, which contained valuable information for each of their brand managers about the success (and failures) of their products, like Folgers coffee and Duncan Hines cake mix. I had a Cincinnati trip planned to attend a convention with some clients from Geisler, a company inolved in seed for birds, hamsters, gerbils, and other pets.

When I arrived in the P&G brand manager's office, he had a proposition all ready: "Have you considered developing a database of your information by product category," he asked.

I had, I said, but it proved to be expensive.

"Well, if you'll do it, I'll be your first customer, and I have a budget of $16,000 for six months of information."

Was I ready for computerization, awkward as it was in those early days of 1965? Since I had $16,000 to answer that question, I set about the business of computerizing the MAJERS book.

Back in Omaha, I told Bill Wurgler I was moving out of his cramped second floor and into larger offices across the alley in the venerable old Woodmen of the World Insurance Co. (WOW) building. This once-grand fourteen-story structure had been the headquarters of the WOW, a fraternal organization that had long since moved into new quarters.

The rent was amazingly cheap: $50 a month. I immediately discovered why. The floor creaked. The walls were streaked with who-knows-what. The ceilings were stained. The windows did not close tightly, and on mornings after a typical Nebraska snowstorm we had to shovel snow out of the offices before starting to work.

But there was plenty of space. We cleaned and painted the walls and I made work tables out of plywood and sawhorses. Crude, but effective. To computerize our system, I needed to set up a key-punch operation with two IBM key-punch machines, a card sorter that would process one hundred cards per minute, and a unit-record processor from IBM. The processor had boards that had to be wired (programmed) to print out the information onto continuous form paper. The job required two part-time key punchers, a part-time operator, and a supervisor.

I hired housewives, working out of their homes, to encode the information, and I contacted IBM and they sent in some smart young people to help me devise a coding system.

It all failed miserably. Looking back on it now, I think we were trying to do too much for those early computers. It just wouldn't come together. Finally, calling upon my engineering background for one of the rare times since graduation, I devised my own system. Again, like the original MAJERS booklet, it was crude but effective.

Within a few weeks we were able to put together in report form computerized statistical analysis of all retail grocery ads in fifty-five markets. This program measured the client's cooperative advertising activity as well as the competition's. Each report was individualized to a customer's particular needs and format. Having given up trying to install my own computers to test-run the program, I contracted out the computers at one of the local supermarket chains. This meant that I had to work on it at the only time the chain had the computer free, from midnight until seven a.m.

I was working at MAJERS twelve hours a day, six days per week; computer operator by night, salesman by day, until I was finally able to hire computer programmers from Omaha's Strategic Air Command headquarters to moonlight for me at the grocery chain's computers.

■ ■ ■

Once I had the MAJERS book computerized, I had to go out and sell it.

In 1966, I decided to approach Pillsbury, mainly because they'd agreed to give me a appointment. This was a cold call, as Pillsbury had never before been a client of ours. I flew up to Minneapolis and set up in a conference room. Ten people from the company filtered in, mostly from the research and brand department. I had a flip chart presentation introducing MAJERS: where we were located, how long we had been in business, etc. Then, I had an enlarged IBM card showing the market, brand, category, advertising retail grocer, the product size, the featured price, and the classification of each feature. Our mission was to provide the best information possible and to develop a weighted promotional index which would allow the client to more appropriately evaluate their brand position versus competition.

As I discussed earlier, we had developed the All Commodity Volume position for each retail grocery market, taking the size of the market (the metro area in each city) from the sales management magazine report. From those readings we could calculate market potential, and, soon, the ad (retail grocery feature) potential. I explained to them the three levels of feature dominance for the advertised items, classified as an A feature, a B feature, and C feature.

I put up four transparencies on an overhead projector showing the Pillsbury staff in two market areas how their brand was performing vs. competition with A and B ads.

It was exciting data and the presentation went very well. I could feel the excitement building in the room. At one point in the presentation, one of the supervisors said, "We'll give this some serious thought!" I thought I had them eating out of the palm of my hand. Once I was done, I even heard a bit of applause.

Then came what would turn out to be a major question.

"Do you also provide this service to General Mills?"

I should have said, "No comment," because General Mills, also of Minneapolis, was their stiffest competitor. But instead, I flashed a hayseed grin and boasted.

"This is a special time for me," I said. "Because when you sign up you will be our *first* customer!"

I regretted the words as soon as they left my mouth.

Their smiles faded. I think someone even sighed.

I had briefly had a bird in my hand, but now I knew it was flying away. I learned a critical lesson that day: Nobody wants to be the first customer of a new, untried product.

■ ■ ■

Pillsbury eventually subscribed, but it would be a year or two (and many clients) later.

From that point on, I told myself, I would never reveal a client to a potential client, or vice versa. This would be a good decision, because in later years we did business for competitiors in hot fights over the same market, showing each side how to win. Each marketing team served non-competing clients. For instance, our Stanford, Connecticut, office serviced Pepsi, our Atlanta office serviced Coke, our

Chicago office serviced R-C Cola, Shasta was serviced in San Fransisco, and Dr. Pepper and 7-Up were serviced in Omaha. But we were up front about this. We never publishd a customer list, and our customers accepted these stipulations *before* they signed our contract.

By then, we could afford to set our own rules. But in 1966, I was hurting for new business. MAJERS was in debt to the tune of a staggering $60,000. I wasn't very wise yet in the ways of the business financing, and if a check for $300 arrived in the mail, I tended to consider that money to be spent for something today rather than applying it to yesterday's bills. The debt finally reached proportions that I could no longer ignore, and I sought out an investment banker for help. His first thought: "Find six doctors to invest $10,000 each."

I didn't want six bosses, even if they let me run the company.

"Okay, how about finding one investor with $60,000?" he said.

I didn't want one boss, either.

"All right, then call each of your creditors and ask them to continue to supply you while you paid off the debt over the next three years," he said.

That made sense, so I followed his advice. It was amazing. All of my creditors had enough faith in me and MAJERS to accept. Most of them charged interest— all except the biggest creditor of all, my printer, Jack Barnhart.

Once I got my creditors to heel, I went searching for investors. A longtime friend, Ray Kopecky, listened to my story.

"I'll give you $7,000," he said. "If you can pay it back great, and if not that's okay, too."

I thought that was a good sign. So I did the most illogical thing: I offered to buy out my partner Bill Wurgler. I wanted to be sole owner of MAJERS, which, of course, meant I'd be sole owner of the $60,000 debt.

"Name your price," I said to Bill, who had paid $5,000 for his share only two years before.

We settled on $15,000.

My lawyer thought I was crazy.

"You're paying $15,000 in order to get sole ownership for a $60,000 debt?" he asked.

"But the debt is my responsibility, not Bill's," I said. "He's no more than a stockholder. I ran the company, and I ran it into debt."

"Okay, but how are you going to raise the $15,000?"

I had quite a plan. I'd sell a vacant lot I owned for $5,000, then raise $5,000 on my life insurance, and, finally, I'd take a second mortgage on my house for $5,000.

Only trouble was, the banker didn't agree with me on the value I placed on the vacant lot.

"I paid $5,000 cash for that lot," I explained to him.

"That doesn't mean it's worth that much," he replied. "Land doesn't have any value until somebody wants to buy it. Don't you know the first law of real estate?"

I said that I didn't.

"Never buy land with cash," he said. "Buy it with borrowed money. Whatever the lender says he will loan on undeveloped land is pretty close to what the land is worth."

Fortunately, the land really was worth $5,000. I sold it on my own to a watch repairer, and as far as I know he still lives there.

With the $5,000 apiece from the insurance company, the second mortgage on my house, plus the $5,000 for the lot, I was able to buy out Bill Wurgler.

After having to enlist partners in my bleach business, Amred, my ad agency and two different partners in MAJERS, I was the sole owner of my own business. That I owed $60,000 to my creditors and was still not taking a cent out of my company did not cloud my enthusiasm a bit.

I had a company, a mission, and a commitment to excellence. It was 1966, and I felt that anything was possible.

THE SHELF OF

The Shelf of Finding Your Market

One of the saddest experiences in business is to create a product the manufacturer believes is great, but that no one wants to buy. Every seller needs a buyer. This adage may seem to elemental to belabor, but creators of new products can overlook this fact in their euphoria over developing something "new under the sun."

This should have been my concern when I developed the MAJERS booklet in 1963. I had no guaranteed buyers. But I knew that the grocery ad pages had a value to me and I was confident it would have a value to others. Today, I might have created focus groups and created surveys to gauge the interest in the product I was creating. But back then, I just went with my gut, which, in many cases, is the best survey of all.

When I sent out the sample books and began receiving checks and signed order cards from everyone from Procter & Gamble to Chicken of the Sea to Winn-Dixie to Sara Lee. I knew I had a market. How big of a market? I didn't know. But I had started something. Just as Procter & Gamble began with candles, and IBM with cash registers, I stood on the tip of something big. Like the original products of the other two companies, MAJERS's original product—the book of grocery store ads—would only be the beginning. Twenty-three years later, the grocery ad booklets would still be being distributed. But by then, it would only be about 2 percent of our company's annual revenue.

In Chapter One, I mentioned the three keys to building a successful business: a mission, a commitment to excellence, and a market. A fourth element in the process is luck. Like someone once said, "The harder I worked, the luckier I got." Mine came in two ways. First, when the brand manager at P&G asked, "Have you considered computerizing the information contained in the grocery ad books?"

Then, the OPEC crisis in 1973 to 1975 changed the way retail grocers and the consumer product marketers viewed the value of the trade promotional expenditure. When that happened, power began shifting from the marketer, whose emphasis was on advertising, to the retailer, whose emphasis was on the merchandising and promotion. The grocery retailers and wholesalers realized their inventory was at maximum levels and marketers began panicking as their inventories started to build. They had to move product, fast. Promotion became critical.

MAJERS was there to help.

I changed the company to fit the times, and MAJERS evolved from a database service to a complete information service that gave both the manufacturer and the retail merchandiser the critical information they needed to move products. Eventually, MAJERS became a consulting business with a vast database of retail features, coupons, and in-store displays matched to daily retail checkout sales information.

We named our complete information service our "MasterTrack" service. Our first customer was Frito-Lay in Dallas. The fee: $1,200,000. We were innovative and were accurate with the millions of bits of information we provided and we began to grow with knowledgeable, experienced, talented, and professional representatives.

From the beginning we were pursuing a new and unique idea: not only providing the client with information on how they were doing, but also showing them how their competitors were faring against them. At what we called the "data stage," the customer would receive the following along with their annual contract: two copies of customized computer reports showing their brand alongside the competition by market, by specific retailer, and by the day of the week, showing the A,B, and C feature activity. Following that, they would receive a key account report showing their monthly and quarterly activity by the key retailer in each market.

In the information stage, our representative was a person hired from the industry. An example: an area sales manager from P&G or a retail grocery merchandiser. On the marketing side it could be the Brand Manager from P&G or a sales representative from the pharmaceutical segment of the industry. We brought experienced, talented personnel to the client, which was a tremendous asset and value.

As we evolved into the intelligence stage of the business, our personnel also had a higher level of experience with the national salesmanager for Clorox, the brand manager from Cheeseborough Ponds and a research director from the industry, all hired by our future COO Frank Schanne.

Our services began to project the A.C. Nielsen share data for each brand. Nielsen reported on a sixty-day schedule. One share point in the carbonated beverage category was worth $100,000,000 in annual revenue. We told Pepsi and Coke the markets and the regions of the country that needed to shore up in promotional results in order to enchance their Nielsen share reporting.

Our service showed the client how to implement the information with the retailers in order to improve their results. Our experienced representatives were the key.

To measure our market became more difficult for us as time went by because we had to create or "force" the marketplace. By that I mean, we didn't just bring out a new product and sit back and wait for the telephone to ring. Likewise, when IBM came out with its first computer, few people contacted them, demanding to be sent a computer—it took IBM's sales power to force the market.

At MAJERS over the years we hired the finest talents we could find to push the ball up the hill, because people are what make our free enterprise system work. Eventually MAJERS staff numbered six hundred in six locations, including seventy-five in Stamford, Connecticut, thirty-five in Chicago, fifteen in San Francisco, and five in Cincinnati to serve the Procter & Gamble account alone.

■ ■ ■

Beyond the power of the MAJERS team, we had some good fortune that enabled us to expand our market. It happened to stem from events that were unfortunate for many other businesses: the recession of 1972–1974 and OPEC's dramatic increase in the price of oil. Across the nation the business climate was sluggish and packaged goods manufacturers turned to a variety of ways to improve their sales. One was to place more emphasis on promotion. This gave our business a big lift.

Freed from the constraints of top management, who often did not fully understand supermarket promotion, marketing managers increased their promotional spending by a considerable margin. This gave MAJERS an opportunity to capture some growth, or, at least, the potential for growth. It was our job to take advantage of the opportunity. At a business gathering, but a social environment, I was visiting with Mr. Jim Ferguson, the CEO of General Foods. We were discussing the GF promotional expenditure which was approximately $1 billion. They had retained earnings or capital reserve of $750 million.

What kind of return do you get on the capital?" I asked Jim.

"We get about 8–9 percent from bonds and some equities," he said. "Mostly secure investment."

I then asked the question that I had been hoping for the opportunity to ask a CEO for some time: "With $750 million retained capital and 8–9 percent return, and with approximately $1 billion in annual promotional expenditure, which gives you the greatest return?"

I was hoping, of course, that he'd say promotions, which would be a boon to us.

"I wish I knew!" he said. "If you can tell us our return in the promotional expenditure, that would be a real winner."

After that, we focued on expanding our service to find the answers.

■ ■ ■

Our first ad collection booklet had created a ripple among the major manufacturers, but we weren't content to offer only that booklet, because there just wasn't enough growth potential in that one small package.

So we began encoding our information into a database service that we called *Totals and Trends*—"Totals" because we offered total "specials" information for the recent period, and "Trends" because we could offer comparative trends for the past year.

I tried, and failed, to sell to Pillsbury. Then, I flew from Omaha to Minneapolis two or three months later for a nine a.m. meeting with the research manager.

"Sir, can I help you?" asked the receptionist.

I said I had come to see the market research manager.

"Oh, he's out of town," she said. "Weren't you informed?"

"No, I hadn't been," I said.

"Well, since you're here anyway, let me take you back. I have another individual who works with him and you can make your presentation to her and it won't be a wasted trip for you."

She led me back to a cramped little room, where the research aide sat with an underling. I played it like the Carnegie Hall of conference centers, giving the full presentation, with charts, displays, everything. When she could see that this was something with substance and meaning, the researcher said, "I hate to interrupt you. But this is far more important than for you just to tell it to us. If you have time, I'll go and see if I can get the vice president of sales. I think he should hear this."

I thought, *Great! I had never gotten an audience with Pillsbury's vice president of sales.*

"He'll see you in his office in about five minutes," the person said when she returned.

I made my presentation to the vice president of sales, as well as his regional manager.

"I'd love to have your service, but I don't have any budget for it," said the sales VP "But do you have time to tell your story again to our VP of Marketing?"

"Of course!" I said.

He took me back to his VP of Marketing and I made my presentation once again. "I'd like to bring in three of our brand managers: one for refrigerated dough, one for cake mixes, and one for specialized products like cookies," he said. "Do you have time to do your proposal again?"

I did it again. Two of the brand managers weren't available. But I presented to one.

"The other two brand managers will be available at 1:30," he said. "Would you mind coming back then?"

"I'll be here at 1:30!" I said.

So I did the presentation once again. I didn't leave Pillsbury until three p.m. I'd arrived with a nebulous appointment. But I left with somewhere in the range of $120,000 worth of business and a very important business lesson: never be rude, never be unkind. You never know what good will come out of your kindness, and you don't know where a bad situation will turn into a great one.

■ ■ ■

I also sold *Totals and Trends* to the Maxwell House division of General Foods and the Sperry Hutchinson Company, distributor of S&H Green Stamps. For *Totals and Trends*, we measured a company's retail promotional activity, individualized by region. We reported the data and could tell the company which of its promotions were working in getting the retailer features and which were not, where the company was getting its money's worth and where it was losing ground. We told S&H which products were featured with their stamp offers.

Let's take Jolly Green Giant green beans as an example. I showed the brand manager how, in Boston, his green beans gained position in 1968 over 1967. They had fewer retailer features in 1968, but Jolly Green Giant green beans were given larger type, great price reduction on features, and more effective store displays in the 1968.

The brand manager already knew his company's financial figures for 1967 and 1968, of course, but he wasn't sure why they differed. Now, with the information MAJERS could provide, he had a better grasp of the elements affecting sales. And, he could plan his promotional events in cooperation with the supermarkets.

But not every department of a company understood the value of the MAJERS service. Because of the difference between sales and research, we almost lost a customer or two.

I usually sold my product through sales and marketing departments, not through marketing research departments. There is quite a difference between marketing and marketing research. The former employs advertising, production, and the salespeople to move products. The latter are numbers crunchers who compile and report statistics to the marketing people. In this case it was the market research director who had purchased our service, for $120,000 a year, but he was not making use of it—or not making proper use of it, as I soon discovered.

He apparently did not see the value of our information. I received a call from one of his people saying they were going to cancel our services. I asked for a meeting with the research director and the VP of sales so I could show him the reasons to retain our service.

This marketing research director had decided his people could do what we did and do it cheaper. I asked his office to send me their research numbers before I flew in for that meeting. These provided me with the ammunition to point out the shortcomings of their own program. They thought their figures would prove their point and they didn't need MAJERS. In fact, their figures proved the opposite. Their approach was to simply have their sales force report retail ad activity. This is like asking the fox to guard the hen house.

For instance, their sales force simply *reported* the A feature from Bob's Supermarket. We did not simply report or audit the market. We *measured* the market and Bob's was not part of our sample since it was only one store. Their sales people were measured on the number of A and B features they obtained during a month. But it was the comparison and display of information, along with the accuracy and timeliness of our system, that made MAJERS unique.

At the meeting, I told the research director, "First, you are gathering your information manually. Ours is automated. Your retrieval system is obsolete, time-intensive, and thereby less effective.

"Second, you've lost objectivity by having your salespeople report retail activity, and objectivity is one of the principal advantages of MAJERS data.

"Third, you're losing perspective on the industry. You collect information about your product but not about all of your competitors. Yet information about the competition is absolutely necessary if you are going to beat them."

I showed them that they were missing the big picture. They were working with a small piece of the market, emphasizing their brands rather than the entire category, and their people were auditing data in a very subjective way, favoring the Maxwell House brand over competitors.

Our service, I noted in conclusion, provided completely objective information on all products in all ads in 102 major markets across the country. In the end, a higher-up in that organization who was wiser than the market research director saw the wisdom of my argument, and renewed the contract.

Some people understood our service extremely well and put it to excellent use. Bob King of General Foods often said that, yes, the company used our data for their promotional expenditures, but they applied the information to many other areas as well.

"We pass your data on to the finance department," he said. "They come to us in the fourth quarter of the year and tell us a particular brand needs additional case movement to reflect better year-end revenue, which, in turn, will allow the company to present a better per-share earnings report for the year-end closing.

"We go through the data and earmark brands that are promotionally sensitive.

"Then through the finance department we get additional promotion dollars which we use to pump into those markets. The results are improved case movement and, consequently, better year-end profit statements."

It was apparent that we had tapped a rich market, but frequently we had to fight to prove to our clients that they really needed us. Doing so strengthened our resolve that we were in the right business. It was our challenge to continue to offer new services in order to keep our company moving forward.

■ ■ ■

As our market became even richer, we continued to expand and reorganize our services. In 1968, we replaced *Totals and Trends* with what we called the *Score Report Service*. With standardized data, we could offer clients a detailed retail advertising accounting, a key account (key retailer customer) and market trends. Detail and trends were reported monthly, the key account quarterly. Now the client could actually keep score on the monthly effect of his promotional dollars.

Part of our improved service to the client came through a bit of luck and some ingenuity. The luck part occurred when Mutual of Omaha was selected by Xerox as one of six test companies throughout the United States for its new computer form printer. Xerox promised manageable 8½ x 11 inch printouts with legible type, a huge improvement over their earlier cumbersome printouts on green paper, which were terribly hard to read and awkward in size, almost impossible to file and retrieve.

Mutual agreed to test the machines for Xerox, but said it would need two machines, one for backup. My friend Bill O'Connor at IBM suggested I inquire about using Mutual's extra printer to reproduce my computer printouts. Mutual agreed, in part because it would give them another example of how it worked, and in part, I think, because they had a soft spot for a beginning entrepreneur. As a matter of fact, Mutual, one of the nation's largest health and accident insurance companies, had been started by a single entrepreneur and is still privately managed. He was V.J. Skutt.

The arrangement was perfect for us. That Xerox printer reproduced those big sheets into handy pages at a cost to us of just about what the paper was costing Mutual. We bought some notebooks, had the name "Score" printed on them, and filed our reports in the notebooks. By this time we were serving the retail drug market as well as the grocery supermarkets—many of their products overlap—and we published our reports in green notebooks for the drug store and blue for the supermarkets.

Our clients loved it. They could use the notebooks for easy reference. This effort gave us a tremendous advantage over the growing number of firms trying to compete with us. The *Score Report Service* showed our clients we were a sophisticated, progressive company. It was a real plus for us. Because we were still a relatively small business doing about $1 million in revenue annually But now we were producing a product that looked like it came from a much larger firm. We were the first into the market with an 8½ x 11 inch report. We beat SAMI, a division of TIME, Inc. as well as the industry leader, A.C. Nielsen.

Not long afterward, we received another assist from an unexpected source, an old fraternity brother of mine, Tom Barrett. Tom had been a couple of years ahead of me at Kansas State, and I often thought of him as a role model. I had studied his test papers, because, like me, he was a chemical engineering major.

Now he was president of Goodyear Tire and Rubber Company.

Goodyear used MAJERS services, but the purchasing agent was the market research director, not Tom Barrett, and as I noted earlier, few market research people had the imagination to make full use of our service.

We weren't earning enough money from Goodyear and decided to drop the company when they refused to sign a new, higher priced contract. I stopped in to see my old fraternity brother and told him our margin was such that we couldn't justify continuing with Goodyear as a customer.

"You talk about margins," he said, "But I think you're making your decision based on the wrong margin. If you focused on helping us improve Goodyear's margin, I would see to it that your own margin is taken care of."

His reply startled me, but was a revelation. Fatten his margin, and our margin would fatten, too. I gathered our marketing and sales people and told them Barrett's comments. From that day on, our sales efforts targeted chief executive officers, chief operation officers, and vice presidents of sales and marketing, not directors of market research.

I also never forgot that there are people other than corporate executives who can help or hinder you, and they work in unlikely departments. Would you believe clerks in newspaper circulation?

We subscribed to all the major newspapers in our 102 major markets, but all too often we received the "Bulldog Edition," or the first of as many as six editions in a day. And very often the Bulldog, which was intended for mail subscribers far away from the metropolitan area, did not include all the day's advertisements. Sometimes the grocery ads, critical to us, were omitted.

When that happened, someone at MAJERS had to call the newspaper's circulation department and request a metro or city edition, with all the grocery ads, to be mailed to us right away. We'd always call the same person at the newspaper, and I soon realized we were leaning on that person a bit. Naturally, some of the clerks got a little irritated with us.

We tried to make a friend of these people. We sent each one a letter and a brochure, apologizing for being a nuisance, thanking them for their patience, and explaining why MAJERS needed those grocery ads. Come Christmas we'd send them a little gift, maybe a personalized desk clock or a pen, something they could use at the office and something to remember us by. They appreciated the thoughtfulness, and we got our ads.

We also discovered in our early days that no matter how straightforward you are to some people, and how much you let them know what you can do for them, they just don't respond.

We got into the banking business early, because we felt it was similar to the grocery business in one important way: there is only so much business, and banks compete for this business just as supermarkets compete. If we could help supermarkets, why not banks? Well, we could help them, but they refused to understand how.

At the time, bankers and savings and loans competed for savings account depositors by giving away things like toasters, blankets, and calculators. They were promoting to attract what is known as the "defined"—or target—market. Figuring this was a rich new area for MAJERS, Dick Chamberlain pursued this idea and we entered the banking promotional information field at the persistence with what we called the *Gold Book*—which, he felt, needed a rich name since we were trying to attract bankers and the savings and loans.

He clipped and reproduced all the financial ads in fifty-five major markets and added a summary that showed what was happening in terms of promotional items. For example, were they giving away fewer toasters and more jewelry, or special trips, or free airline coupons? Wouldn't banks in Nashville like to know what the banks in Seattle were doing to attract new depositors?

We did line up a number of customers, but never enough to make it profitable, so we dropped the service. Although the grocery trade eagerly bought our service, banks never quite warmed up to us. The difference between bankers and grocers is that grocers were then, and still are, far more sophisticated in their consumer marketing. Grocers have been marketing to the consumer for years, and they understand the consumer. Bankers and savings and loans, even today, do not always seems to understand their customers.

The most sophisticated banking operation we encountered was Bank of Minneapolis (now Norwest Banks) and the operators of several banks in Nebraska. They had a marketing department that would go through our *Gold Book* and really digest and act upon it. But they were the exception in the financial field.

We failed in other markets as well. We tried to duplicate our supermarket success with a variety of hard goods, including automobiles, tires, chain saws, small electrical appliances, and motor oil. But the short-sightedness of bankers and savings and loan executives was duplicated by many hard goods manufacturers. These people are inventory-oriented, not consumer-oriented. Inventories are the prime consideration in every marketing device they use. Toyota was so different from Nissan in its business operation that a standardized report was impossible. Each auto manufacturer wanted an individualized report, and we couldn't charge enough to make it worth our while.

While in theory it was logical to adapt our services to other businesses, in practice only the grocery and drug packaged goods businesses were sophisiticated enough to understand and utilize our data in a benefitical way.

The supermarket field might have been our best customer, but it was a pretty impressive customer. We had found our market.

 **THE SHELF OF**

People, Relationships, and the Birth of the MAJERS Corporate Culture

People are what make our free enterprise system work, and that system is a unique and precious concept. To be able to live in an environment where free enterprise is possible is both a privilege and a challenge.

Beyond a ready market, I believe our employees were what made MAJERS a success. Richard Dupreye, chairman of Procter & Gamble, said, "If you take away our people you would ruin this business, but if you took away our facilities and our capital but left us our people, we would rebuild it all in a decade."

It's a great feeling to have outstanding talent working for you, and the best entrepreneurs are those who realize the importance of hiring people with vastly more talent than they have. We didn't just hire the traditional man (or woman) in the dark blue suit. Our employees came in all shapes and colors, but if you could figuratively take them apart and place them under an X-ray, all would have some characteristics in common: good relationship skills, strong egos, and exceptional courage. They were hard workers, results-oriented competitors.

At first, this was by instinct.

But it soon became a science.

Through that science, we created one of the greatest marketing teams ever assembed in American business.

■ ■ ■

At first, however, I hired without science, relying, instead, on luck.

After doing much of the computer input work myself in the wee hours of the morning on the Hinky-Dinky computer, I turned to some friends, IBM computer experts who were working at SAC headquarters, for advice.

"Support staff," they said. "You desperately need support staff."

I took out a newspaper ad for part time computer encoders:

"Wanted: Women to work in their home.

"Needed: Accurate detail work, responsible to schedules, and paid on a per-piece basis.

"Send resume: MAJERS. All replies will be answered.

The ad netted seventy-one responses—all of them acceptable candidates. I hired the top five, but we needed a supervisor. Then, one day, Bernice Peterson walked in, and, almost immediately, she began saving the day. (Every business needs a Bernice Peterson, someone who, despite neither founding nor owning the business nonetheless considers it their own.) She walked into my drafty office in the worn-out old Woodmen of the World building and, overlooking the circumstances, said she was ready to start, immediately. I hired her on the spot and, rising from computer encoding secretary through various positions, Bernice Peterson served MAJERS for more than twenty years. She was around fifty and had worked for General Mills. She seemed to know what I was trying to do at MAJERS. She said her husband was ill and she needed a job.

"I can only promise you half days now, but I'll try to extend your hours as we grow," I said.

She took me up on the offer, worked one half-day, and from then on was full-time. She became my right arm.

The women Bernice would supervise had children and wanted to stay at home and make some extra money. They were college graduates and some had been doing detail work in their homes: typing envelopes, addressing labels, light book-keeping, and telephoning.

Bernice and I called the five best candidates for the encoding work. After our brief meeting to explain the work and its pay—three cents per recorded data card—I told them all, as a group, "You're hired."

Pretty soon, we had thirty women working from their homes, each working an average of thirty hours a week and bringing in income for their children's education, to help support the family, or for luxuries they couldn't otherwise afford. We bought a small van and once a week we delivered the newspaper ads for a particular market to each of the women. They studied the ads and encoded that information by hand, which we picked up and fed into the computer. Each coder had a workstation in their home so they could lay out the ads. Each retail ad had a different format, and therefore you could not do it by measured size. It had to be determined by dominance in the ad. It was a trained judgment call and it worked very well. They were smart individuals and were very accurate with their decisions.

Once the coder's cards were punched they were run through the computer audit program for an accuracy check where a certain accuracy would yield the coder a bonus for that week's work.

In addition to the housewives encoding work, the good Catholic nuns at Cathedral High School sent me three or four of her brightest boys to paste up grocery ads for the weekly booklet.

As we grew, we were able to hire all seventy candidates who replied to our original ad.

From beginning to end, MAJERS had predominantly female employees. Data collection became a very important segment of the business, even though it was done on a contract basis, almost immediately growing from six to sixty contract workers and then the IRS stepped in to challenge our "contract" status. Since we couldn't supervise our contract laborers work at the minimum-wage level of compensation, we added additional space and moved the women who were willing into our facility. We lost about 25 percent of the group, but we were able to add others, resulting in a data processing staff of more than a hundred.

When the social security challenge came, I wanted to know how our compensation of three cents per card compared to minimum wage. I called one of our top processors, Marge Behn, and asked, "Marge, have you determined if our compensation allows you to earn minimum wage?"

"Why do you want to know?" she asked, guardedly.

I sensed she didn't want me to reduce her payment per card.

"The truth is we make a lot more than minimum wage," she said.

■ ■ ■

By 1968, our computer needs had grown beyond our abilities, and I began looking for a full-time programmer. I found a programmer at Northwestern Bell Telephone Company, whose title, "Computer Systems," initially excited me. But I learned very quickly that the title was an illusion: Northwestern Bell gave all of their programmers that title so that others would not hire them away.

He worked for us for about six months when I learned he had programmed the computer reports to average the averages. That meant if the market average was 10 percent for Detroit and 20 percent for Chicago and 30 percent for Minneapolis, you can't report the district average to be 20 percent. You must go back to the detailed facts in each market to calculate the district average. When I approached him about this he didn't understand what was wrong with that. That is when I said, "You're fired."

My next hire, also in 1968, was Bert Davis, a smart guy from Guarantee Mutual Insurance Company. After about a year Bert came to me and said, "I quit."

"Why?" I asked.

"The hours are too long and, honestly, I just don't want to work this hard," he said. "I'm going back to my old job."

I turned once again to my friend Bill O'Connor at IBM, and told him I needed a great computer expert, immediately. I was in Chicago, signing up Sara Lee, and called the office for messages. "You have an urgent call from IBM in Omaha," said the receptionist.

"I've found the perfect guy for you so when you get back I'll give you his name and background," said Bill O'Connor. "I've told him about you and your company and he's interested."

His name was Red Byars and he was a demanding electronic data processing manager who had built a data processing operation from scratch at the University of Nebraska in Omaha. Red was looking for a challenge. Since 99 percent of the computer systems in Omaha were IBM, he was already familiar with the equipment and people. And since IBM'ers like to help their users find other jobs within the IBM family, Red was eager to meet me on the recommendation of my IBM friend Bill O'Connor.

"We are a ship under construction and not a luxury liner at sea," I told Red at our first lunch. "The hours are long, the challenge and opportunity is great, and the business is exciting."

"When do I start?" Red asked, adding, "I never watch a clock, I watch the calendar."

The Texas-born retired Air Force master sergeant made good on his word. He was the most dedicated worker a young company could hope for: a taskmaster, whose red hair matched his hot temper. "Red, I always listen to what you have to say, but I never listen to how you say it," I'd say when he'd come into my office to blow off steam.

Red drove an old car he never washed, and he always parked it on the street curbside in the No. 1 stall outside our building. He parked there because he was always first at the office, usually by 6 a.m. Red's old car usually remained in its parking space until he went home, anywhere from 8:30 to midnight. One day a secretary looked out the window and saw a tow truck hauling away Red's grungy old car. We hurried outside to see what was going on. It turned out the owner of the dry cleaning establishment across the street had called the police to have it towed away.

"That old car is there when I open up my shop, and it's there when I close," he said. "It's so battered and dirty I just assumed it was abandoned. It never occurred to me anybody would work those kinds of hours."

Once Red explained that he did indeed work "those kinds of hours," the tow truck was unhooked from his car.

Bernice Peterson and Red Byars had a loyalty to MAJERS that went far beyond their paychecks and a forty-hour week. Their belief in the company was such that, by the time of their deaths, the two buildings we occupied in southwest Omaha were named the Peterson Building and the Byars Building. The plaques are still on those buildings.

■ ■ ■

In 1969, I was MAJERS's only salesman, traveling cross-country and signing up companies including Coke, Pillsbury, General Mills, Quaker Oats, Kraft, Kimberly Clark,

Pepsi, S & H Stamp Company, General Foods, and more, companies whose locations spanned North America.

It seemed like I spent a third of my time dozing in an airport lounge chair—a piece of furniture never designed for a restful night—waiting for the snow to stop falling, for an aircraft replacement part, or the arrival of a connecting flight.

MAJERS, in those early days, could barely pay for the airline tickets, let alone spend the major bucks required for an airplane of our own. So I made my weekly calls to the travel agency in Omaha, which, I think, counted on us for their quarterly profits.

For a long time, not only was I the number one salesman, I was the *only* salesman. My schedule called for me to leave Sunday evening, usually for the East where most of the packaged goods manufacturers were headquartered. In 1965, I stayed in the garment district at the Lancaster Hotel at 38th and Madison, where my contact at General Foods returned my call.

"How much do you pay for a room and where's the Lancaster Hotel?" he asked me. "I've lived in New York all my life and I've never heard of the Lancaster Hotel.

I said it was a clean room at a reasonable price and was convenient to my work.

"You can raise your overhead by $12.50 per night and your image by a thousand percent if you stay at the St. Moritz," he said. "Ask for a court room. You won't have a view of the park, but people will think you know what you're doing."

My routine was to check into the St. Moritz, and probably remain there until Friday noon. With my toys from F.A.O. Schwartz in hand for the children I'd fly back to Omaha for a 6 or 7 p.m. arrival, but my first stop would not be home. It would be to the office. There I'd pick up the production Dick Chamberlain had been gathering for the entire week. Dick was my first "executive." He was in charge of all the part-time and full-time employees who collected information, and he would have it all neatly catalogued for me on my arrival Friday evening. I'd then go home to my family, but not for long. When the Omaha supermarket chain computers finished their work for the night, somewhere between 1:30 and 2 a.m., the security guard would call me and I'd drive out to the computer office and enter our data. That night I'd be fortunate to get two hours sleep. Sleep was the variable. With deliberate scheduling, I could average five or six hours of sleep a day for the week, but that meant some shorter workdays in New York.

And who ran MAJERS while I was living in air terminals, coach seats in crowded jets, and look-alike motels? And was it being run properly?

The staff was doing its work, efficiently and expertly. I was the only one selling. I was the only one delivering the numbers, and I expected them to deliver the product. And they did.

I never worried about what was happening back in Omaha. I knew our people had a real commitment to their jobs, and I gave them ownership of those jobs. I never told them how to do their work. I only outlined what they were expected to do and let them find ways to do the work. That's how a support culture works.

As the only salesman it was my job to get MAJERS on a solid footing by acquiring major clients. I brought General Foods into the fold. I also sold Coca-Cola, Pepsi, Lever Brothers, Pillsbury, Green Giant, Quaker Oats, Hunt Foods, and others. I was a good salesman—for me it seemed like a form of recreation—because I loved it. I was confident we had a product that would help the clients make money, and if I couldn't sell a marketing or sales vice president it usually was because he wasn't smart enough to understand our wares. That may not sound very complimentary, but it's the truth.

Hunt Foods, one of our early customers, thought it could stay ahead of us. Their vice president of marketing, Al Crosson, took me on a tour of the company, pointing out in one office how ten or twelve employees were busily extracting information from our weekly booklets. Hunt Foods subscribed to several copies of each issue, and their employees were extracting the information manually.

"See?" Crosson said, "We're already doing what you're trying to sell us."

The product I was trying to sell at the time was our new computer-generated SCORE Reports.

"But you're paying nearly a dozen people to do it," I said. "We're doing the same thing by computer, which ensures an accuracy that pays for itself over a period of time. Not only that, we're giving you trends, something your employees know nothing about."

I continued: "Buy our SCORE Reports and protect the objectivity of your information. Then I won't need to jack up my price for your subscriptions to the book because that's your source document."

He smiled, knowing I was speaking only half in jest. He bought the new service because he realized our computerized way of cataloguing information was far superior to his manual method.

Once we opened field offices it wasn't necessary for me to travel as much. Our field people made the calls, and they were superb. Where I had been content with a $20,000-a-year contract from Coca-Cola, they would land a $200,000 contract, and, subsequently, a $1 million contract.

That was tremendously exciting for those young men and women and myself. They'd never sold a million-dollar contract before, and neither had I. In fact, they hardly thought such figures were possible when we first hired them.

As the field sales people took over more of the selling, I was able to cut my work week from eighty hours to a more respectable sixty hours. Most people go to work about eight o'clock in the morning. Make that nine in Manhattan. Or sometimes seven in Omaha, at least for some CEOs I know. In any case, the twelve-hour day means getting home after the kids have eaten dinner, perhaps while they're doing homework, or it can mean they're already in bed.

Saturday afternoons and Sunday until departure time were the days I had available for my family. Through my first marriage I have three children: Kris, Lynn, and John, and I made an effort to do things with them. They loved going out to dinner with just me, and not just to fast food joints, but to a nice place where they would dress up and study a fancy menu.

We often picked an expensive downtown restaurant, and when they were little one of their favorite things to do after dinner was to ride the outside glass elevator at the Hilton Hotel, now the Red Lion Inn. It was kind of scary, but they loved it, huddling against the one solid wall and looking out over the lights of the city to Council Bluffs across the Missouri River.

As they grew older, I'd often take them out to dinner one at a time. My kids didn't realize how hard I worked, but they knew I loved them. In 1970, I wanted to give the kids a way to enjoy the summers, so I bought the shell of a two bedroom cabin from Floyd Mellen for $8,000 on a small lake west of Omaha. I budgeted $2,000 for finish materials, such as wall paneling, bathroom tile, carpeting, refrigerator, stove and furniture. I did all of the finish work during the weekday evenings and the weekends. I'd get some help from the kids but they were usually busy swimming, sailing, and water skiing.

This kind of schedule eliminates the chit-chat about everybody's day at the dinner table. It cuts out playing catch in the backyard, and it kills any chance for a bedtime story. Those young years go fast, and pretty soon the kids aren't kids anymore. They're teenagers, and they have their own agendas that may not often include Dad.

You do have some time in the morning, but morning time is a hassle, with brushing teeth, taking showers, grabbing a bite to eat, and hurrying off to school. Nobody gets very close to anybody during the morning rush hours. As I look back, these are the times I wish I had been smarter in managing my schedule. It's better to spend the dinner hour at home than the breakfast hour.

So I adjusted my twelve-hour day. I made time to become a father and a friend with my kids. It's far better to let them go to sleep on loving, caring thoughts than to forget what you've said before breakfast.

When I knew I was leaving for a business trip, I'd draw a picture on the countertop of a guy flying off to a new city. It looked like "superman" in flight. The caption would read, "I'm off to New York but I love you very much, Dad." One time I baked sugar cookies in the shape of letters that spelled each of their names so that they would see them at breakfast and know I loved them.

The twelve-hour day remained important to my contributions to MAJERS for a long time, because time was the finite resource I could provide; if you don't have money you give time. I could have gone to the bank, perhaps, and borrowed capital to hire more people, but in my entrepreneurial stage I hadn't yet learned how to manage financial resources. Dick Chamberlain managed himself and the few others in the home office while I was out selling, but it wasn't until I was able to spend more time in Omaha that we were able to expand to the point where we needed managers and supervisors.

Sometimes, it seems, I took the office with me on the road. Take the example of the fire. It occurred in the late 1960s after we had moved from the Woodmen of the World building to a shopping center in west Omaha. It was a modest center, and we had our office on the side farthest from the street, next to a Japanese restaurant called Mount Fuji.

The fire started in a gift shop on the far side of Mount Fuji and spread to the restaurant. Excellent work by the fire department kept it from reaching our office, but smoke and water damage devastated our place. All our backup data cards were stored in the basement, and when the fire wall gave way, water flooded into the space and washed those cards all over the floor.

It's kind of hard to find humor in a situation like that, but there was one bit of it: A card for a tuna company was found lying on a pile of the restaurant's wet noodles. *Tuna and noodles!*

The morning after the blaze, we held an impromptu meeting out in the open air of our terrace. Our office was a terrible mess and we had only two choices: fold up and go our separate ways, or reorganize and start over again.

Without exception, the staff chose to start over. They were saving their jobs of course, but more than that, they wanted to save MAJERS. My first assignment was to find a new location while the others dug in and tried to create order out of the chaos in the basement. We both succeeded, and that's when we moved into space above the pet products company.

But I had another assignment. We had lost beyond recall important data from a number of markets, including Canton and Akron, Ohio; St. Louis; and Dallas. For several weeks during my travels I would go to those cities' public libraries and study newspaper microfilms, laboriously copying grocery ad information that had been lost.

It was tedious work and it required dedication on my part, but, as the company owner, I could hardly show less dedication than my employees. And we duplicated our records and completely recovered from the effects of the fire. I've been blessed with high energy and amazing stamina, and these certainly were put to serious test by that fire. But our insurance check totaling $43,000 was a great help to cash flow.

I had been told that if you build the organization, the organization will build the business; by the late 1970s the business was built. Consequently it wasn't necessary for me to devote twelve hours a day to the business. We had competent employees doing that during the normal work hours.

My contributions to MAJERS consisted of cerebral things—planning, strategy, policies, keeping an eye on the balance sheet and on our performance measurements, plus managing our board meetings. I set the pattern and others met the standards. I attended the monthly planning meetings, but the executive vice president ran the meetings.

■ ■ ■

I was still traveling constantly and solicitating new business. After the outlining sales offices were established, I developed our Canadian clients. The majority of my sales trips were to develop the Canadian market with Pepsi, Quaker Oats, Kimberly

Clark, Kal Kan Pet Food, General Foods, etc., where many of the U.S. grocery products companies had their Canadian home offices.

In 1969, O believed it was time to consider opening our first field office, it would be in the East, right? Wrong. We put it in the San Francisco area. The reason we selected San Francisco is because a competitor had shown up on the scene, taking our ideas and some of our business that we had developed in the Bay Area.

I selected the West Coast because I was convinced I would find better job applicants there. Jobs went begging in New York City. In the Bay Area, people waited in line for good jobs.

Seeking a West Coast regional manager, I turned to Stanford University's placement center. They came up with Reginald Rhodes, whose grandfather had founded a grocery distribution business, and he opened our first field office in Redwood City, California.

Reg's job was to service the few accounts we already had in California and to solicit new business. He was so successful that when it came time to open an office in the East, in Summit, New Jersey, I chose Reg to handle it. Reg was an outstanding sales talent. The VP of sales at Dole Pineapple told me, "He is the most graciously persistent guy I've ever met."

Opening our branch in San Francisco cost us $120,000, but we got our investment back in a year and a half.

■ ■ ■

By 1974, we were a company of almost three hundred employees, far too many for me, personally, to have hired each one. But the matter of adding the right kind of people to our workforce was a great concern of mine.

I'd always hired people by the resume and gut instinct. If they had the experience, and I could connect with them in some way, they got the job. Later, some of the people in my various busineses liked to double-check people by their astrological signs. We had a book, *Linda Goodman's Sun Signs*, that shows us the trend for personality. But you don't want to base a multi-million dollar decision on astrology. We needed something more, something powerful, and something provable.

I found it one day in the place where I found so many things: *The Omaha World Herald.*

The article stopped me right in the middle of breakfast. It was about a company in Lincoln, Nebraska, called Selection Research, Inc. (SRI). The company's president, Dr. Donald O. Clifton, spoke of measuring people's potential in ways I'd never heard about.

Clifton talked about people in new ways, about "developers," people who take satisfaction out of each increment of growth in the business or in the employees; about "arrangers," people who specialize in organizing human and physical resources for maximum productivity; about "relators," people who build rapport with employees; and about "delegators," and "activators," and innovators." He said his company specialized in identifying each employee, or potential employee, by SRI's classification, and then putting them into positions where they could maximize their strengths.

Immediately, I put down the paper and called Owen Neary, a local businessman I knew from church. I remembered that he had said something about working with a revolutionary personality profiling firm in his Data Documents business—and he immediately said it was the same company I'd read about in the newspaper.

"We have used SRI for the past five years and have found it to be very valuable, but also quite challenging," he told me.

Owen suggested I stop by his office to review the results Data Documents was experiencing from SRI's intervention. He said SRI interviewed, tested, and labeled prospective employees three ways: "conditional," "recommended," or "highly recommended." He said a conditional person might be good for $500,000 in annual sales, a "recommended" would generate $1 million in sales, and a "highly recommended" could bring in $1.5 million. It didn't work every time, but often enough that my friend was impressed. Very impressed.

Immediately, I wrote a letter to SRI's president, Dr. Donald O. Clifton.

A week or two later, a Dr. Jim Sorensen of SRI called me and suggested we meet to discuss working together. We met in my office. Jim had a PhD in psychology and was very outgoing, with a good sense of humor. I asked about the company and how it got started.

"Both Don and I were professors at the University of Nebraska and, along with another PhD, we recognized a need to measure an individual's potential for success as a salesperson," he explained. "We approached Mutual of Omaha Insurance Company and they underwrote the development of the SRI approach. With the

Mom and Dad in their bakery in Osage City

Mary Amelia Scribante

Otto Joseph Scribante, Sr.

A.J. in front of the house in Osage City

Dad in the navy in World War I

A.J. as a junior at K-State University

Otto Jr. and Adrian (A.J.), 1942

A.J. in the U.S. navy, 1949

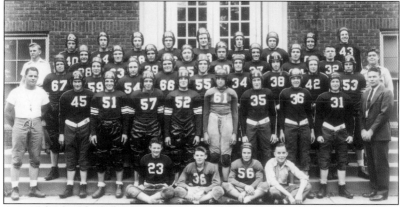

Osage High School football team: A.J., #53 and Chuck Ford, #57

Mom's cake, decorated by her son

Mom's birthday at 83 years old

Composite Market Survey (later changed to Grocery Ad Book)

This Week in Omaha magazine at the time of purchase

The Grocery Ad Book

A.J. and Ben Foley and Dorothy Lynch
Salad Dressing

IBM Unit record equipment with
four in-home coders, 1965

1965 original in-home coders

1966 in-home coders

Brite*Eyes bleach

Brite*Eyes bleach label

Midnight shift with the IBM contract programmer on the 1440 computer

The original office in the WOW building

Jim Sorensen, PhD and physicologist

Bernice Peterson

President's Cup winner John O'Keefe, 1980

Stamford Office,
1010 Sumner

Red Byars and
Jeanette Norenberg

Walkway of the new
headquarters building

Gerald Collins at the groundbreaking for the new headquarters, 1983

MAJERS Corporation groundbreaking

MAJERS reception in the original building

Mike Allen

Marge Behn

George Beaumont

Warren Conner

Dave House

Jim Howe

Gary Parkhurst

Frank Schanne

Ray Johnson

Red Byars

Charlene File

Dick Chamberlain

Tom Wilson

MAJERS's first computer, the IBM 360, Model 20

Leadership conference

Bill O'Connor, Bob Sander, and A.J. at the Free Enterprise Man of the Year Award for A.J.

MAJERS Plaza, 42,000 square feet

MAJERS headquarters

Computer tape storage

Darlene Fox

Rich Olson

New headquarters reception area with the receptionist, Joanne Howland

MAJERS complex in Omaha

MAJERS advertising

MAJERS Brochure

On the left, Bill Wyman and on the right,
Marty Mulholland

Group portrait of the Stamford office
team: (left to right) Larry White,
Ron Foisy, Frank Schanne, John O'Keefe,
and Dick Schaefer

Group portrait of the Chicago office
team: (left to right) John Mason,
Bill Harless, Steve Fremarek, and
Chuck Harris

Campaign chairman for $2.6 million fraternity house remodel

Uncle Sam played by A.J. for the STRAT COM military recognition awards

Flight in the F-14 Tomcat fighter plane–Top Gun School

A.J., a governor of Aksarben at the annual ball

A.J. and John Elway

A.J. and Sunny at St. Patrick's Cathedral in New York

A.J., Sunny, and President Bush in the White House at a tribute to President Eisenhower

Aug. 25 - 1990

RONALD REAGAN

Dear A.J. & Lynda

In the hustle and confusion of the day in North Platte I feel I didn't properly thank you and "Ak-Sar-Ben" for your handsome gift or for all that you do and have done for me and for the causes we believe in.

Please know that I'm aware of your contributions and service in so many ways and am deeply grateful to you both. I take our paths will cross again and often. We shall treasure your gift.

Sincerely Ron

President Reagan's note

success they were able to demonstrate, and with satisfied clients like Mutual, we were able to grow on a national basis."

He said they like to interview the top eight people at the company as a first step, to gauge the level of existing talent at the company. "The reason we do it that way is to learn if we can work with the company," he said. "If the talent isn't strong enough then we'd be wasting our time, because they will not appreciate our value and the ultimate turnover would cause management to terminate the relationship."

I signed up immediately, and Jim interviewed my top staff members and me.

"You already have some very good talent at MAJERS, and it's obvious that you would appreciate the value of our service," he said.

It was the beginning of a long and prosperous journey.

■ ■ ■

"SRI begins with the concept that everybody has a God-given talent for something, everybody does at least one thing well," Dr. Clifton told me. "If there is a means by which we can identify talent in a person and then provide the person with the proper training, encouragement, challenge, and environment, then that person ultimately will be more successful than if we match him or her with tasks they don't do well."

In other words, he said, play to a person's strengths. Don't try to pound a square peg into a round hole just to salve your own ego. None of this "because I said so" nonsense. Don't put a person in a job where his or her weaknesses will guarantee failure.

He said SRI's psychological interviewing would identify those talents in potential employees—and we'd immediately see the results. The first step was to bring their people into our organization and let them learn about our culture and environment as well as the idiosyncrasies of our industry and of the chief executive. The second step was the employee "interview," consisting of a set of structured questions that, when answered, would provide Dr. Sorensen with a basis for his analysis. One of the questions dealing with ego might have been:

"Your church is raising money by selling ties. You sell far more ties than anyone else. When the announcement is made that the church exceeded its goal, there is no mention of the fact that you sold the greatest number of ties and raised the most money. How do you feel?"

The ego-driven response might be, "I'm angry and very disappointed. I'll never sell ties again. Either that, or I'd stand up and ask the group, 'Who sold the most ties?'"

Ego isn't a bad thing, Dr. Jim Sorensen told me. But when you find a person with a very large ego, but without the balance of courage to go along with it, you will find someone whose communication frequently has to be interpreted to be understood.

Some of the questions on the SRI interview were open-ended. For example, "Describe for me a good salesman. Describe for me a good manager. Tell me the advantage of being the sales manager, versus being the salesman."

The responses to these questions and many others reveal the potential of the individual's success as a salesman and as a manager.

Each interview was taped and the results were sent to Dr. Sorensen for analysis. Before long, we had every employee—and ever prospective employee—run through the SRI interview process, and we made many changes—all for the better—in assignments after the tests were done.

Then, Jim Sorensen and I hit the road in search of talent. We ran ads in the local newspaper and would conduct interviews in adjoining hotel rooms, me in one room, Jim in the other. I would greet the individual then give them to Jim to interview. He could score them on the spot and when he found someone uniquely qualified for a specific job, I would take over, beginning the relationship that would lead to a trip to Omaha, and eventually, a job.

One example of the incredible success of SRI's process was Frank Schanne. We met him in White Plains, New York. Halfway through his interview, Jim excused himself and came in my room. "This guy is an exceptional talent," he said. "He is someone you can build upon and he will help you grow this business. Plus, he knows your industry. He's a perfect fit, if you can hire him."

Frank's talents included: great courage, ego, development, competition, ethics, sophistication, stamina, empathy, focus, the ability to win others over to his way of thinking, communication, influence, responsibility, and integrity. Without SRI, I would have had to go on hunches. Now, I knew exactly who he was and where he'd best fit.

Frank Schanne had the talent, the industry knowledge, the experience, and the love for the business. He acquired this love from his father who was the head buyer and merchandiser for Thriftway Foods, a large retailer in the northeast. Our Summit, N.J., office had a real need for good leadership. The day before Frank was to join us, I called him.

"Frank, tomorrow will be a great day for you, me, and MAJERS. I recall you shared with me that you welcome the challenge of growing the eastern territory."

"Yes, that's right," he said, enthusiastically.

"Okay, I need you to fly to Chicago tomorrow morning and meet with me and three account guys from the Summit office to discuss the leadership needs," I said. "The manager that was there is out of focus and I need your immediate help."

"I'll be there," Frank said. "You can count on me to do whatever is needed."

Those words to me were like the beginning phase of the Battle Hymn of the Republic. "Mine eyes have seen the glory of the coming of the Lord ..." That might be stretching it a bit, however there was great pressure on me to resolve the Summit problem. I had four young client service and sales individuals and an ineffective manager. We met in a United Red Carpet conference room at O'Hare Airport. It didn't take long for the account guys to define the problem. The plan was to terminate the manager after Thanksgiving. This meeting was on Sunday, November 7th. Two days later I received a call from Frank. "A.J., you need to come here and fire this guy immediately. This Friday will work," he said.

"I'll be there Thursday," I said.

Frank picked me up at the Newark Airport and we had dinner to review the next day's plan. Next, I met with the research manager, John, and told him, "Your performance is very disappointing to me. You're married and your moral standards do not match those of MAJERS. Your leadership style is ineffective, and therefore, you are fired. Please clean out your desk and leave the office before noon." We had the locks to the office changed and hired a security guard to be sure we had no repercussions.

Frank went to work with his belief in the selection tool of SRI and his concept of what organizational disciplines would be needed in order to provide the clients with service that would meet and exceed their expectations. He once told me, "I believe turnover of employees is unproductive. I have witnessed a few great managers who have had no turnover and great success. My plan is to recruit and retain individuals with the right talent and experience for customer service."

"Frank, I have great confidence in your character and your exceptional talent," I said. "Your knowledge and experience are what is necessary to build the eastern office into the shining star it can become under your leadership. The eastern part of the country has the majority of the CPG headquarters and holds great potential for MAJERS growth. I know you will get the job done. You have the responsibility and the authority and the opportunity to have some fun along the way."

He visited General Foods and Pepsi to observe how the information was being used. At General Foods it was not being implemented very well. But Pepsi valued the information, and the potential was much greater. This experience confirmed his belief that it will take unique individuals with talent and the experience necessary to get the information off the floor, out of the boxes, and into the boardroom in front of the top management of the client company. Frank developed and implemented his strategy.

"General Foods will be an anchor client as will Colgate, Cheeseborough Ponds, and Pepsi," he said. "With success, the word will get out, our reputation will be known, and then everything will open up."

While he was an employee at Scott Paper Company, Frank went from a successful start in sales to being the manager of corporate staff employment. It was there that he learned about recruitment advertising, search firms, and interviewing. He told me, "I believe I can achieve the necessary recruiting. When you add SRI to this belief it is a natural fit."

For General Foods, with a world-class product management organization, he hired Warren Archer who had his MBA, some sales experience, and came to MAJERS from Nestle where he was a highly respected product manager.

For Colgate, Bill Wyman had a successful sales management career at P&G and later was a sales manager for one of the nation's largest food brokers. He was the perfect fit for Colgate. Bill was a perfectionist and could handle the challenge of the Park Avenue New York client.

Dick Schaefer was a perfect fit for Cheeseborough Ponds. He had both product management and sales management in his background. He also came from a health and beauty aides (HBA) manufacturer, Richardson Vicks. Dick became a star with his clients.

Pepsi was an extremely demanding client. Bob Sander was the VP of sales and Frank worked for Bob at Scott Paper Company. Frank said, "At Scott Bob surrounded himself with extremely bright people who knew the value of information. I knew I had to find individuals who could keep up with the demands they would make."

The addition of Larry White, a professional market research manager who was one of the best in the business, helped to fill that need. In addition Larry taught Frank's team how to best analyze the information for the greatest value. Later Frank made Larry the VP of marketing for MAJERS.

Then Frank hired Bob Schmitz, market research manager at American Can Company. He was a great addition and a quality individual. Next, we found Mike Allen from John O'Keefe. They had worked together at *Reader's Digest*. Mike had just received his graduate degree from the University of Pittsburgh and was the perfect guy to take over the Pepsi client from Larry. Mike was from San Francisco and since that office was underperforming, Frank worked to train Mike on Pepsi and eventually Mike would be the west coast VP. Mike's father was a very well-known management consultant and gave his son a lot of talent and sophistication. Mike was a natural.

In Frank's own words, "Getting to see the president of our clients was a critical step in developing the client."

After thinking about that I hired John O'Keefe who had an advertising and sales background from *Reader's Digest* and was the very best at developing relations with top management. A.J. Scribante and John were two individuals that solidified our reputation with top management early on, and later others did the same.

The word was out that we were good and MAJERS was an exciting place to work, earn, and grow. I would join Frank in Summit at the beginning to be a part of his quarterly business reviews and planning sessions with each east account team. They were each treated as the professionals they were and Frank believed that you "inspect what you expect."

The Chicago office managing the central and western regions had a team made up of Steve Kingsbury, the regional VP, supported by Steve Fremarek, Bill Harless, John Mason, Chuck Harris, and Sharon Janelle. While the eastern office was developing, Steve and his capable team made up the shortfall in the revenue plan. It was a great team effort.

When Frank became VP of sales for the nation, he was instrumental in developing each office to the same level of performance. Later as the COO he incorporated this style by developing ten key indicators of management in each operating department known as KIM numbers that were reported monthly. (Key Indicators for Management)

With great personnel in place, we were well-staffed to handle the forthcoming growth of our business. Once client management was properly positioned I quickly focused my attention on the needs of our information gathering by being sure we had great talents in place.

The data entry operation was computerized to both receive the input keyed into the terminal by the highly trained operator who reported all of the information about the retail feature and then entered their judgment for the A, B, and C ad classification.

When a client would visit our operation and ask a data entry person, "How do you know what ads are A, B, and C?" the answer would be, "I code the same ads from the same markets week after week and I am very familiar with their format. Therefore the judgment is very consistent and very reliable. The information then passes through the computer audit program to check for overall correctness."

The clients are always impressed with the quality of individuals, the level of technology that has gone into the coding system. We eventually ran two shifts for data entry, computer generation of reports, and Xerox form printers to reduce the size to 8.5 x 11-inch notebook-sized reports.

I'm proud to say that the coding system I developed myself after the IBM approach failed is still being used to this day. I always looked for the simple solutions to complex problems and this is one that has worked well. My chemical engineering professor that flunked me in organic chemistry would be pleasantly surprised.

When someone is fiercely competitive and blessed with a balance of good talent and gentlemanly grace, good things happen—particularly when they have a sales quota to reach.

In 1981 at our annual year-end celebration at Pebble Beach in California, I presented the President's Cup to that year's top performer, Mike Allen. Afterwards, Dick Schaefer came up to me and said, "A.J., these trinkets don't motivate me.

Just keep paying me my commission checks and I'll keep producing for you."

"That's good to know, Dick," I said. "However, I'm counting on you to keep up your good performance."

"You can count on that," he said as he walked away.

Dick's competitive spirit was great, but it was hidden under his gentlemanly behavior. Guess who won the President's Cup the next year at the Amelia Island year-end celebration? Dick Schaefer. And guess who began to relish winning it? After receiving the award, the cup and the usual 'Thank You' check, Dick turned to me. "Has anyone ever won this two years in a row?" he asked.

"No, Dick, no one ever has," I said.

By now, you can probably guess who won the Cup the second year running, at the next year's conference. Of course, it was once again Dick Schaefer. At this event, he turned to the audience of his peers of Client Service Managers and said, "Who can beat that record?"

No one did. But they sure tried.

"What do we need to do to enhance our productivity and our ability to perform as this business doubles in size?" That was my question at the weekly management meetings with all of the department heads present. About fifteen in total were all in town.

We leased larger and faster computers from IBM along with more disc capacity, faster tape processors, and larger data storage devices. "We need a 4341 computer dedicated to just the data entry," Jim Howe, the manager, requested.

"It would be nice if we had our own Xerox forms printer so I no longer have to send people out to Mutual of Omaha to use their equipment," was Dick Chamberlain's request.

The decisions were made at the table when possible since each manager was given the responsibility and authority to know their needs in order to fulfill their part in the corporate mission.

Because of SRI, I knew their potential at the beginning of our relationship, when it counted most, and in this way it became an integral part of MAJERS culture. The SRI testing results were so precise that our employees gave Dr. Jim Sorensen a nickname, borne perhaps out of him and the results of the interview with one of them to determine if they would be a good hire—an interview so thorough that he could practically see their bones.

They called him Dr. Death.

■ ■ ■

SRI developed a profile of success for our company, and, as we began hiring people to realize that profile, our productivity began to skyrocket. We wanted people with what we and SRI called "high gestalt"—a driving desire to complete things or the ego, courage, desire for development, competition, ethics, stamina, etc. The ego was the driving force towards personal significance. Courage was a value system: of firmly believing in right and wrong. Development was the key ingredient in management, both in terms of people and clients. Competition would lead to achievement. High ethical standards allowed one to weigh various forces and always do what was right. Stamina would be to stick with the task at hand, much like perseverance.

We hired people who had a need to complete whatever they were working on, from extracting figures from a newspaper ad to building a sales organization. Once high gestalt people get a task, they can't sleep until the task is completed. We sought out people with that quality; we hired and nurtured them.

All MAJERS supervisors and managers were required to use SRI's testing methods. A lost employee was a tremendous cost since another had to be trained at considerable expense. Our retention rate increased dramatically with the addition of SRI.

When Reg, who headed our West Coast office, left the company, I looked for a replacement. I'd hired Reg the conventional way, but I'd find a replacement using the science of SRI. Dr. Jim Sorensen and the following ad, which I ran in *The New York Times* and *The Wall Street Journal*:

> "Do you have the talent to maintain quality in a growth environment? If so, come to the White Plains Hotel for a personal interview with Dr. Jim Sorenson, a psychologist. You may have the opportunity to manage people, and sell a unique service to Fortune 500 corporations in the Consumer Products Industry. Call for an appointment."

One hundred-fifty responses poured in, and Jim and I thought one stood out: his name was Frank Schanne, and, after testing him, Dr. Jim became very excited. "He's a real find," he said. I invited Frank to join me for dinner, where I made him an offer to join MAJERS, which he immediately accepted, until I mentioned the salary I had in mind. Much too low for Frank Schanne. But we stayed in touch.

That Christmas, I sent him a card, and he called me the day he received it.

"Would you consider coming and making a presentation to our sales team explaining the value of MAJERS's service?"

Of course, I said, and the presentation went well. Frank was impressed with our growth over the past year. We went to dinner where he then expressed his interest in joining the company. By then, I could afford a higher compensation and hired him on the spot.

It was the beginning of an incredibly successful relationship. His talent proved to be as Jim's analysis indicated, if not even better, and I learned another lesson: you've got to pay the price to attract, and keep the best, but salary isn't the main factor in retention.

■ ■ ■

With our incredible growth, we rapidly outgrew a small business's simple personnel processes of basic medical claims and employee roster maintenance. Since I was head of human resources in addition to my other responsibilities, it became apparent we needed a person in charge. In December of 1978, I hired Judy Woodard to be my administrative assistant. It was apparent that her talent could be used for a more important function, and so we moved Judy to develop personnel functions. Then, when she told me she felt underutilized, I made her the head of that department, asking her to turn the skeletal operation into a significant human resources department. She agreed—on the condition that she be properly trained. While overseeing the installation of sweeping changes she set up a two-year plan during which she attended workshops and seminars, took classes at Michigan State University, and researched human resource professionals in Omaha.

Our new human resources department, which Judy Woodard created, would expand to encompass the recruitment and hiring of people and their technical training, growth, development, and productivity. The department would establish hiring practices and pre-hiring tests, guidelines for promotions, compensation rates, and equity in compensation. And she would work in close contact with SRI and with the management of MAJERS. Our director, Mr. John Cleary, was the chairman of the compensation committee of the board.

Sometimes, SRI helped us keep employees that supervisors wanted to let go. A good example was when Frank Schanne told me, "I need to fire Bill Wyman."

"Before you do anything, I want you to go and meet with Jim Sorensen and discuss the matter with him," I said. "We spend far too much time and money finding great talent, and we need to gain all of the insight we are able before we let someone like Bill Wyman go."

Bill was a client service/sales representative for certain clients and had a sales quota to achieve for his area in the east. Jim studied Bill's SRI interview and told Frank, "You would be wasting an exceptional talent." Bill wasn't making sales calls as the result of his low self-esteem, resulting from his past experience.

"He just needs some successes and he will be one of your best sales managers," Jim said.

Sure enough Frank set up some calls whereby Bill could make the sale, and, sure enough again, he began feeling more confident in his sales skills. Bill Wyman became one of our top salesmen and marketing managers.

SRI conducted more than five thousand interviews for MAJERS during a five year time period from 1981–1986. Some lasted forty-five minutes, some up to two hours. Those efforts were directed mainly at determining a person's talent and ability to perform the tasks required for the job vacancy.

Personally, I conducted one hundred or so interviews using the SRI questionnaire. From this experience I was able to gain great insight into a person and found the process to be very valuable as we evolved. We paid SRI for each employer analysis report, each quarterly employee survey, and each new hire they brought to us. Within a couple of years, we were one of SRI's best clients with monthly payments of approximately $25,000.

SRI was a great vehicle for employee selection and placement, but it also became a management tool. We created a four or five page report on each new hire, outlining their strengths, their talent, and their potential for success. Judy Woodard took the process to much greater heights, working with each department to add the necessary—and specifically suited to the position—talent as we grew. Whether hiring from the outside or promoting from within, we based our employee recruitment on a triad, or triangle, system. One side of the triangle was concerned with talent (identified by SRI), the second side with knowledge-skills ability, and the third side was called employee chemistry (human relations with managers and supervisors). We went through an evolution with our supervisors and managers. In the first stage we synthesized the hiring process, bringing all responsibilities into the central office.

One day, John O'Keefe, our eastern region vice president, told me that he could do an equally good job of hiring without SRI.

"Okay, John, try it on your own and let's see how it goes," I said.

Seeking an administrative assistant, he hired the way the men have hired since time began. Not by science, but by appearance. She was an extremely attractive blonde. Six months later, he came to me and said, "I've come to realize the importance of SRI."

When the woman's work began sliding, John had her go through the SRI testing, so he knew how she fared in the area of strengths, which revealed that she was a classic round peg in a square hole. At the time he terminated her, John was an SRI convert, realizing the duty of a company to see that every new employee becomes the best that they can become within an organization by determining their potential on the "front end."

We sought out people who were highly professional, talented, with experience, dedication, and a commitment to excellence. We wanted people eager for responsibility; people with courage who would stand their ground and challenge management if he or she felt a challenge were necessary.

Then, once we found the perfect person, we took the next step: we paid them well and recognized their every achievement.

■ ■ ■

High-performing individuals—whether salespeople, electronic data processing programmers, data gatherers, supervisors, marketing analysts, or others, thrive on appreciation and recognition, be it compensation, commissions, or bonuses. Identification of a person's strengths and perfect placement strategies all come to naught without the recognition and appreciation for the person. The paycheck is further down the ladder. Having suffered through all of my low-paying jobs, I realized this early on and created a profit-sharing plan as soon as MAJERS had a profit to share. Each year I put both cash and company stock into the plan. Each year-end, our employees received a rendering of their value in the plan.

Select management individuals could also purchase stock in the company on a cash-for-shares basis. We created an incentive program, in which they could pay 50 percent in cash and then the company co-signed the loan for the balance with a local bank. The bank held the security until the loan was paid. Ownership, I quickly learned, is a powerful incentive and a great motivator.

We found other ways to create corporate pride. Each year, we had a "Founders Day" gathering, a high-energy gathering where we issued plaques and diamond pins for five years, ten years, fifteen years, and twenty years of employment. We recognized special achievement with checks and letters of recognition. To develop family pride in MAJERS, I'd bring in a professional counselor from California who conducted a three-day seminar enlightening the teenaged children of MAJERS employees in five key areas, including independence, self esteem, empathy for others, responsibility, and the importance of choosing good friends (and, later, business associates). I learned that when a company can positively influence the children of the employees, it immediately raises the productivity of the parents.

As MAJERS grew, my job became one of direction and leadership. Each year I would set the objectives for the year. The managers would then break those goals down to each department. We implemented an outstanding benefits program that allowed us to compete and bring in talented and experienced people. We installed across-the-board compensation plans involving salary ranges. For the first time, people began to feel there was equity in their paychecks pay.

Our job descriptions and the pay scales created a compensation system that was based on integrity. An honest and forthright approach that use the paycheck as a fair and equitable incentive. By installing a "Performance Appraisal System," that focused on objectively evaluating and rewarding performance, we created measurements for every department and tied performance to compensation. "Do more and you get paid more," became the new rules of MAJERS. Raises and promotions were given on the basis of an employee's performance. Once we moved to a results-oriented system of rewards, our productivivity soared.

■ ■ ■

The hiring continued through the 1970s: exceptional people, exciting growth, more sophisticated service. We never tried to convert a technician into a sales rep. We hired great sales talents from the major food producing companies—regional sales managers, field sales representatives, or national sales people who were interested in a new challenge.

As CEO, I spent about 35 percent of my time interviewing potential employees until I had fourteen managers reporting to me. It became apparent that I needed to form a management organization. The first step? Delegate responsibility and authority. I moved Frank Schanne to the COO spot. He took over the sales offices and assembled a powerful sales and marketing department and forming the client service function by hiring and training marketing analysts who would process and analyze the information in support of the marketing executives.

We hired the top CPG marketing graduates from St. Joseph University. Each year one of the executives would make a presentation to the senior class. Afterwards, a few of the seniors would come to us interested in the analyst jobs. One of our hires from St. Joseph in Philadelphia was Ellen Casey, the daughter of the next governor of Pennsylvania. Like everyone else who came to MAJERS, however, Ellen Casey had to get through the toughest part of the process: surviving the interview with Dr. Jim Sorensen from SRI.

We continued to build our sales force and by 1979 we had about forty-five salespeople in a forty-eight-state area selling the MAJERS services and servicing each client to help them better manage their growing promotional expenditure.

The grocery industry was exploding. In 1979, the retail food industries totaled $225 billion, growing at 10 percent from the previous year. Manufacturers were constantly programming their marketing efforts to counter growth in the fast food industry through pages of newspaper specials an in-store displays. The food industry's promotion expenditures had grown from $1 billion a year to $4.5 billion in 1978, with companies like Procter and Gamble spending $400 million annually. But the giants were no different than a thousand other companies: both needed to know what specials grocers were giving their brand versus what their competitors were getting.

To stay on top of the marketplace that was getting more competitive by the day, the manufactures turned to MAJERS.Within three years we would have a staff of three hundred, ranging in talents from computer specialists and statistical wizards to PhDs in marketing, crackerjack sales people, and ex-brand managers of products such as Folgers Coffee, Nestlé Quik to Terri Towels. They all had different talents yet were connected by their egos, courage, pride, and commitment to excellence. SRI enabled us to identify these people and put them in positions where they could excel. I had found the secret to success: that people, not policies, make a business great.

THE SHELF OF

Leadership

Somebody once said that a leader is a person who will take you someplace you've never been before...nor have they. Or, as *New York Times* columnist Tom Friedman has said, "Leadership is telling people what they don't want to hear, not what they do want to hear."

A leader is a courageous innovator and motivator, one who has the mental power to create a vision and the practical skills to bring that vision to fruition. A leader is committed not only to the end result but also to the people involved, and is willing to take a risk in service to the vision.

When I started MAJERS I didn't want it to be just another research company. I wanted this company to be different. I wanted to be the best, not just for the recognition of my company and myself but to build something of substance and to give recognition to the many people who made it happen.

The true leader of a nation, a private enterprise, or a family realizes that the success of leadership is dependent upon the growth and development of those who are led. The stronger the individual in any group becomes, the more fully that person is able to develop his or her character, and the stronger the leader of that group becomes. Leaders become builders of people by example and through education, and in return they grow significantly themselves.

We hired with an eye for leadership, seeking those with a concern for people as well as a concern for productivity. We always *over-hired* because of our focus on growth.

MAJERS grew significantly from 1974 to 1979. We implemented the SRI hiring system and were assembling an organization of exceptionally talented people. Sometimes I wasn't sure if I was leading them or running from them, with them leading me. They were that good!

I discussed that the four stages of developing a corporation demand different kinds of leadership, each stage illustrating a progression in management styles.

The four stages include:

• The entrepreneurial stage: Crisis management.

• The personal stage: A personal approach to management.

• The professional stage: Management raises the bar by hiring professional managers. Fairness and equity are implemented into the operation of the business.

• The bureaucratic stage: The company develops its policies.

Tom Wilson, the senior partner of McKinsey and Co., the management consulting firm in New York, shared the four stages of a company's growth with me. I made note of them; I had already passed through the first two and was experiencing the third. His concept was very enlightening so I embellished upon the idea with some guiding detail derived from the real-life experience.

As the company's founder and leader, I was determined to keep MAJERS from sliding into the bureaucratic stage, when policies frequently matter more than people. But we did advance through the other three.

In the entrepreneurial stage, the founder/manager/workhorse (me) moves from crisis to crisis. He is always putting out fires. He doesn't plan; he reacts.

I began as a doer. The books needed to be mailed, so I mailed them. The newspapers needed to be clipped so I clipped them. The solicitation list needed to be formulated, the phone calls needed responses, and when the *Miami Herald* didn't arrive on time, guess who had to run down the right person to have it airmailed? Me. The one who owns the business handles crisis management in the entrepreneurial stage. It was *my* idea, *my* dream, and *my* talent and perseverance that were being called upon to get the initial job done. If the founder hangs in there and the business begins to succeed, then it's on to the second stage—the personal stage.

In the personal stage, more people are involved in the running of the business. However, the company remains small enough for the manager/founder's style to remain personal. He has time to plan and to get to know the employees. There are few titles; everybody works shoulder-to-shoulder. And when an employee has a personal problem, the boss—and not the human resources department personnel—usually finds out about it and offers help.

From the very beginning, the people I hired at MAJERS were both co-workers as well as friends. When a fire destroyed a colleague's home, our data processing expert Red Byars helped get the family relocated in a motel, made sure the insurance people were contacted, arranged for school transportation, and did other necessary and helpful things. My company and I offered moral support to our colleague in that time of crisis, and it was a MAJERS family effort to help the family get back on their feet.

Later, Red told me, "I did what you would have wanted me to do and said, 'Since we are all part of the MAJERS family, we will always take care of each other.'" No policy required, just a lot of heart. Everyone from the department pitched in and turned a crisis into a caring act for the entire family. That's the essence of the personal stage—which, with a company's growth, is very hard to sustain.

In the professional stage, it's easy to lose the camaraderie of the personal stage in certain areas of the company. As I said before, management raises the bar by hiring professional managers. I've discussed the two embryonic stages of MAJERS, so let's move on to the third stage. By this time, the company is usually substantial enough to be plagued with the common problem: copycat competitors. As the growth of MAJERS began to accelerate in 1971, the professional stage became a reality.

I made a sales call on Del Monte, and was told by their director of research, "We don't have a need for your service since we are already doing what you do."

"Could I see your process?" I replied.

"No," said the Del Monte rep.

The next time I was in San Francisco, I asked to see one of Del Monte's brand managers who told me, "We have a company locally that does this work for us."

When asked for the company name and he said, "Brand Action."

I looked up Brand Action in the phone book and invited the two principals to lunch. The men were both newspaper advertising space sales guys. They told me a bit about what they did, which sounded, suspiciously, just like what we did at MAJERS.

"How did you get the idea for your company?" I asked.

"Well, we copied your idea," they replied, finally.

They were using a contracted computer service, just as we had been previously. I didn't get mad that they had taken our idea; I got interested.

"If you ever want to sell your business, please call me," I said.

That was 1969, and I stayed in touch with them. No word. In 1970 I sent them a Christmas card that read, "Don't forget to call me." They called me on January 3, 1971. We had a brief conversation about the business—not much detail about the clients, just some general cost information.

"What were you hoping to sell the business for?" I asked.

"Come out and we'll talk about that," they said.

I knew their sales were $150,000 per year. Their costs were incidental since we had the computer capacity and employees necessary to take over their operation.

Before flying out to San Francisco, I called the bank to get a three-year loan for $120,000. Our balance sheet was weak but I convinced my banker to lend me the money by showing him how we would be performing after we integrated Brand Action.

Next, I called my attorney. "Jim, you and I need to go to San Francisco to buy a company," I said.

Jim would play the bad guy, and I would play the good guy in the negotiations.

We offered $120,000 for the purchase of Brand Action. Two days later, on February 15, we owned the company. I asked Red Byars if he needed to go to San Francisco to integrate our operations. "All I need is a couple of long distance calls with their contract computer service," he said.

Then I turned to Dick Chamberlain, a reserve naval officer who had been with MAJERS since 1965. I asked him to go to San Francisco and close down Brand Action. I gave the company's client list to Reg and Steve and put together a small brochure introducing the company and our people with their pictures and brief background. Brand Action's clients were pleased with the change to MAJERS, as the previous company's service had been erratic and not very accurate. They were not as sophisticated as MAJERS in terms of what they were reporting. It was very basic, but still a great addition for us. We acquired Colgate, Del Monte, several other HBA companies, and paid our loan back in eighteen months.

Red was so excited he took the Omaha staff out for a drink to celebrate the acquisition. Next, we opened our Chicago-area office in Naperville, Illinois. We moved our rep from San Francisco to Chicago and hired a salesman from Pepsi to take over the San Francisco market. Then, two more individuals joined the eastern office and Reg Rhodes left to join Booz-Allen in New York.

By 1978, our quarterly sales for each of our 187 sales employees had exploded to $1,085,000 (from $503,109 per employee in 1975). By 1979 I had more than I could handle well with three remote sales offices, a growing EDP department, the expansion of the number of data coders, installation of work stations to support the data entry terminals, computer editing, twenty-four hour computer report generation, report reproduction via computer forms printing, analysis presentation preparation, establishment of a quality assurance department, management of the equipment leasing function, human resource needs, and the establishment of our outside board of directors.

I was fully challenged with fourteen managers reporting to me. Even with capable and professional help and guidance from our corporate officer and administrations assistant, Darlene Fox, MAJERS was paying the price for developing a lack of good communication and effective leadership. "Success equals talent times the sum of relationship plus clearly stated expectations," SRI's Jim Sorensen once told me. I was stretched way too thin.

Searching for help, we interviewed people from major corporations: Procter & Gamble, Scott Paper, *Reader's Digest*, General Foods, Coca-Cola, Pepsi, and others. Headhunters were calling and we placed ads as we searched for talent. Our new hires were very skilled and well-trained but they didn't know each other and, in the beginning, we didn't know them.

We added more supervisors and managers and, like the new hires, they didn't know the company or each other. They weren't aware of personal matters like an employee's house fire or someone's child with a drug problem. When another employee experienced a house fire, her new supervisor was not around.

As we were growing, we were establishing a management style of fairness and equity. This was also helpful in determining who would receive bonuses and commissions. We were hiring people who had more expertise in their fields than I did, but I had to lay down guidelines for their performances. I needed help, advice, a way to make MAJERS, with its explosive growth, feel and run like a family.

My management skills had come through my own on-the-job training. Now, as we moved through the professional stage of management, it was necessary for me to become a manager of managers for the first time.

I turned to SRI. Their psychological testing indicated I could probably handle the experts we were hiring without my ignorance becoming too obvious. But I needed a formal analysis, just like most of our employees had experienced, to gauge my strengths and weaknesses.

On July 19, 1974, Dr. Jim Sorensen reviewed my SRI analysis. In brief, the four-page report stated: "Mr. Scribante is a sincere and positive person who can be quite forceful when there is something he strongly believes in. His early childhood experiences were typical of people who have the talent to sell and manage other people."

"In conclusion, Scribante does an excellent job of passing an acid test of management—*negativity*. He is secure enough in his ability to manage that he does not overreact to it, even when people criticize his ability to manage. He is sensitive enough to almost always seek out the causative aspects of employee error before responding, which is excellent. He possesses many of the moves of the successful managers we have studied. His goal is to create a more sizable business, something he may feel he can achieve as long as he can continually solve the numerous problems that exist in any growth-oriented operation. He does need to focus more consistently on the best talent available to carry out this growth plan and make a commitment to their development."

I learned something important from that evaluation: I had to let go. I couldn't do it all. I had founded MAJERS, but now that it was in its professional stage of growth, it belonged to an entity bigger than me.

My management approach was simple: to find and hire the greatest talents and the most exceptional people. I would get them properly positioned then challenge them with realistic goals and objectives, giving them the freedom to succeed, and then I would recognize and reward their accomplishments. As a result of their SRI developmental appraisals, I would, in many cases, know them better than they knew themselves Any challenge we set forth for them would not be greater than their considerable ability.

"Growth comes from challenge, not from comfort."

And as we grew, our year-end meetings at Pebble Beach, California; Amelia Island, Florida; or Cape Cod, Massachusetts; provided rest and relaxation along with much-deserved recognition and camaraderie between the various offices.

The key in the professional stage is a management style that features fairness, equity, and freedom. Moreover, at this stage we had to develop policies (or guidelines, as I preferred to call them). A great many of our new hires were in marketing and sales, and those of us in top management had to decide who got a car allowance and who didn't. We had to answer questions such as: What were the compensation policies? How much salary was base pay and what were the performance requirements for bonuses? How were we to compensate non-sales personnel who naturally weren't eligible for commission? Some of our positions were structured on a normal eight-to-five schedule, and others were organized much differently, so we needed a system that would adequately recognize the people in every aspect of our operation. I didn't make these decisions entirely on my own, but it was ultimately my final word on decisions that affected the lives of our people. They had to be weighed carefully.

Roger Harrison, a management consultant from Berkeley, California, maintains that the task of good management is "to release people's personal energy in the service of the organization." In a seminar that I attended, Harrison said that after a long period of relying mainly on technological advances to improve the product and profit, businesses finally are realizing that the time has come to make the employee a partner in that technology. That's what we did at MAJERS, and that's what helped us grow into the next stage.

I've saved the fourth stage of corporate development, the bureaucratic stage, for last because, as I've said above, it's the stage I like the least. In this stage, the policy manual runs the company. The challenge at MAJERS, as elsewhere, was to remain in the professional stage, with just enough policies to let everybody know what the rules were, but not so many that we took away a manager's dignity.

We have all experienced the time when we were told by a customer service person, "We can't do that. Our policy doesn't allow it." But at MAJERS, where the customer is king, the response is, "Tell me what you need and I'll see that you are taken care of."

I discovered that when we hired people who cared about pride and service, and when these people were positioned properly, trained well, and recognized for great work, we could avoid the pitfalls of the bureaucratic stage and avoid hiding behind a policy book. We had individuals who truly wanted to fulfill the customer's needs. Our slogan was, "Making our best work for you."

One day in the late 1970s I received a call from Dr. Roy Stout at the Coca-Cola headquarters in Atlanta. As Coke's director of market research, he managed the budget for information research. This, of course, included MAJERS, a service I had personally sold him several years before. "I'm calling you," he said, "because your VP, Rich Olson, is sitting across from my desk right now and he expects me to accept a 50 percent price increase for next year's budget. Our policy is to accept a maximum increase of 7 percent in price."

Rich Olson had my full authority to increase the Coke price. Our sales and marketing managers had "pricing authority" along with the responsibility to achieve the profit goal. But it was my job to see that the price justified the job.

"Roy, we have known each other since the day I received the initial order from Coke several years ago," I said. "So let me ask you: has our service level exceeded your expectations? Have we always responded to your needs with a sense of urgency, without nitpicking you on price?"

"Yes you have," he said, "But I still can't accept more than a 7 percent increase."

I told him that each year we review Coke's contract, just like we reviewed every contract, to be sure we were achieving our profit margin on each.

"Roy, this is not a price increase, this is the next year's contract price based upon the level of service that Coke expects from MAJERS," I said. "We are no different than your auditing firms or your outside legal advisors who base their next year agreement on the level of service required. We are not a manufacturer whose product's value to your company stays the same year after year. This is not a price increase, it is a new level of service contract based upon how we responded to your needs last year and how we anticipate the level of service you will require in the next year."

By not responding like a bureaucrat, but instead like a professional, we got the increase. The strength of the VP in charge of the Atlanta office, the service we rendered, and the support that we provided helped considerably in getting that new contract approved. It was not policy; it was professionalism—plus a long-time relationship and clearly stated expectations that brought forth success.

When you hire people with great egos and also great courage in addition to the other attributes, they instinctively know what is right. They have the courage to defend and achieve the desired and proper outcome. If we had developed a policy stating: "No one is allowed to involve the CEO of the company in any circumstance," we would have stifled talent, limited freedom, and lost good people.

Not long after the Coke incident, I accompanied Bill Wyman to Colgate. I went to the executive offices and asked to see the CEO, Ed Foster, only to be told that no one was allowed to express even appreciation to him for the business that our company enjoyed with the brand. The company was a very bureaucratic environment at the time, and we were not able to speak with the CEO. We worked to ensure that this never happened at MAJERS, and to dignify both management as well as the operational positions.

When does a company move from one stage to another? There is no exact science, but there are measurements, one being annual revenue. I would estimate that we were in the entrepreneurial stage until 1973, the time when we reached about $5 million in annual revenue, and in the personal stage from that point until we reached about $15 to $20 million. The professional stage starts around $20 million and can last forever if you are able to avoid the bureaucratic stage, as Quaker Oats, S.C. Johnson, and other mainly family-operated companies have managed. In my experience, the bureaucratic stage usually arrives when annual revenue approaches the $50 to $100 million range.

■ ■ ■

Throughout all of the four stages of management and leadership, authority must attend responsibility. A good example of this is MAJERS's relationship with the United Way campaign, which I headed in Omaha in 1985. In that situation the campaign chairman had a position of responsibility with some authority assigned and some assumed, something which I discovered the hard way.

When I accepted the chairmanship of the United Way, I was offered the choice of having a goal of between $10.5 million to $11 million. "This way you can claim victory and still have the celebration," I was told. I decided to have a firm number as a goal that everyone could aspire to achieve. Then we could really celebrate the victory. I chose a high number—$11.2 million—which, if we succeeded, would mark the first time $1 million would be added to the record of previous years.

Jim Robinson, the CEO of American Express, was the national chairman of United Way that year. Omaha's United Way staff was very well-organized and trained, so I had great support. I told them I wanted them to meet with each of the twelve to fifteen team leaders and have them determine a hard-number goal they could each deliver. Then I suggested we meet as a group in the large training room at MAJERS.

I shared with them a few funny and appropriate jokes about winning. Then I had each leader go up to a flip chart and write the number their team would achieve. When we finished, the total came to $11.2 million. We were on our way!

Every two weeks, we had a meeting to report their progress against their individual team goals. In between each meeting, I would be called upon to meet with various groups throughout the area—some eight to ten in size, others fifty to a hundred in size. My mission was to ignite their imagination about the importance of giving back to the community and helping those in need.

One week before the victory party, I was $150,000 short of our $11.2 million goal. I phoned the CEO's of five different local corporations to request (okay, *pled for*) their added help. Just in time, the last commitment came in two days before the big celebration where Jim Robinson would be in the audience. We had raised $11.25 million for the United Way agencies, a wonderful charity that help so many people.

It was my experience at MAJERS that allowed me to really tackle this goal. And we could not have made it without my teammates in this effort, the CEOs of the Union Pacific Railroad, Mutual of Omaha, First Data Resources, Kiewit Construction Company, Northwestern Bell Telephone, and several others, who each contributed a great deal to our effort. The Omaha business community was dedicated to supporting the United Way, as are businesses in most American communities, and they assigned bright, talented people to work on the campaign.

But the campaign chairman does not pay their salaries and has little leverage in case they shirk their duties. The chairman's only management tool is leadership. He must be able to stand up in front of several hundred campaign workers and communicate leadership: forging a path, directing, motivating, and stimulating people toward the common goal.

Delegation, according to my SRI profile, was my strong suit. Over the years at MAJERS I had learned how to relinquish control over many of the duties, and I had learned how to trust others with those duties because I knew they had the talent to get the job done. At MAJERS I learned to recognize people with great sales talent. I searched those talents out in each United Way team, and then I focused on them. I challenged them, told them how good they were and how I was counting on them to get the job done. They did just that.

The United Way campaign reached our $11.2 million goal. Not as a bureaucracy, not by policy, but dollar-by-dollar, person-by-person—the way great businesses, campaigns, and charities are the most successful and most fun. On the night of the celebration, it seemed like all of Omaha was in the audience. I shared some emotional stories and passed out plaques and certificates. I repeated the verse I used before each group I met with during the campaign. "In search of God, I climbed the tallest steeple, but God declared: 'Go down again, I dwell among the people.'"

I returned to MAJERS as a leader in the eyes of the management and the board of directors, none of whom had ever been a United Way chairman. Suddenly, people from the community would come up to me and thank me for my great work and knew me by name.

■ ■ ■

Just as I was striving to keep my own office free from the cursed fourth stage of management, it was also my responsibility to make sure the company's other managers did the same. Managing managers, while one of the most challenging leadership roles, is also one of the most personally rewarding. As the boss, I was more or less in a position to control movement up and down the corporate ladder. A business, in order to grow, must be a mixture of both new faces with their new ideas and old hands who remember how we did things last year. You can't make a gin and tonic without both gin and tonic, and the CEO must be the bartender who makes the proper mix. After the managers come the board members, who, if left to a free reign, can install policy, or bureaucracy, into a company.

Just like the United Way campaign required a coalition of different talents and different committees to make it work, a company needs a diverse board of directors. Establishing a strong board is as important as selecting a talented work force. Board members bring to a company their own experiences, personalities, and styles. They create a balance and supplement the skills and ideas of management with their wisdom. But the CEO must be committed to considering seriously every board decision. You owe this to them. Besides, they are more often right than wrong.

In 1972 our first outside board of directors was established with the appointment of two board members: my brother-in-law who was a banker and my lawyer. The members allowed me to learn the way of a board. We reviewed the quarterly reports and the performance of the company. I sold them "B" stock for cash and paid them $10,000 a year for their service.

In 1976 I realized that MAJERS had outgrown its service of the initial two board members and I needed to replace them. The terminations were made easier since each one would receive a check for $14,000 for the purchase of their stock. "Your valued contribution has helped to bring us to this level of growth," I told each of them. "Thank you. I am retiring your board seats and I am pleased to present you with this check. Thanks again for your good work."

I approached Bill Strauss, who had grown InterNorth from $200 million in revenue to $4 billion during an executive meeting in Omaha. "Would you consider making a speech to my group and share your national and international economic insights and then be a panelist to field questions?" I asked.

He said he would. That evening, before the other directors and our talented team of thirty, he was hooked.

The next day I shared with Bill more of our information and he called me to say, "I am proud to accept and I'll do all I can to help you grow this business."

My first new board member was John Cleary, who founded a business with Omaha's Warren Buffett, and grew it at a significant growth rate until sales were just under $100 million when they sold the company. I had received John's sage advice for several years prior to my invitation. "It's very important that your board is compatible with each other," he had said. "Be sure they bring value to you and the company." That turned out to be great advice, which I followed.

Since MAJERS was becoming known in the community as an extremely successful growth company, none of the board members would tell me "no." But I needed a group of people that could provide honest and thoughtful guidance for the company. The board knew I could override their advice, but they also knew that if I didn't pay attention and respond appropriately they could—and would—leave.

Many closely held companies operate with a board made up of employees, and a few token outsiders who are there because they're either relatives or golfing buddies of the boss. Those boards don't generate much controversy, energy, maturation, wisdom, or fun, and the boss goes along making the same mistakes year after year—or until his creditors close in on him.

I didn't want that to happen to MAJERS. I organized a board dominated by strong outsiders, all successful business and professional men in their own right. These members included:

John E. Cleary, Omaha, an entrepreneur whose company, Data Documents, grew from a $163,000 operation to a $75 million per year operation in fifteen years before he sold it to Dictaphone.

Richard A. Westcott, Des Moines, whose experience was in banking and investment banking, CEO of a chain of discount stores, and a 7-Up bottler.

Willis A. Strauss, Omaha, chairman of the board and chief policy officer of InterNorth Inc., formerly Northern Natural Gas and later known as Enron, a natural gas pipeline company, who serves on the boards of four publicly held companies.

James L. Koley, Omaha, a lawyer whose law firm serves clients throughout the nation and is principally involved in bond issues, mergers, and acquisitions.

The other important thing I learned: listen to others, seek outside advice. I was eager to listen to my board, irrespective of whether I agreed with everything they said. I wanted them to challenge me and I always tried to listen impartially, digesting and, in most instances, acting on their advice. They were a working board, compatible, and wholly committed to the company.

Our first formal meeting was preceded by a dinner at the Omaha Country Club. Most board members knew each other, but not well, so it was a chance to become acquainted. They were joking with one another and asking, "How did he ever get *you* to join this group? It certainly wasn't the pay!"

The first meeting was organized by the corporate secretary, Darlene Fox, who was the consummate professional, which pleased the board. I directed the meeting by having each of the seven VPs present their budget and operating plan for the New Year and comparing it to the previous year.

As John O'Keefe addressed the board meeting, he said, "I was so excited to make this presentation to this revered group that when I got in the car yesterday morning to go to the airport I forgot to open the garage door and drove right through it! So now you know how excited I am to be here."

THE SHELF OF

Long-Range Planning

In the entrepreneurial stage of MAJERS, I never had time to plan ahead. I reacted from crisis to crisis.

In those days, we were never sure what calamity might strike next. The newspapers might not arrive on time, the bank balance might be short, making it impossible to pay the printer for the last week's work, or the housewife data-input "technician" handling the Wichita market survey might have a sick child and fall behind in her work.

Fortunately, we enjoyed more winners than losers, more days when things went right than when things went wrong. Then, around 1971, I was wrestling with the big question of whether to be tax-oriented or earnings-oriented. That might not seem to be a major crisis, but it was a very big decision, and like so many seemingly small choices, would have a big effect on the growth—or stifling—of MAJERS.

In 1969, when MAJERS first started showing a profit, my accountant, Shelly Broadsky, raised the issue of corporate tax options. "Have you thought about whether you plan to make stock available to the employees?" he asked me.

"Yes, but I don't have a plan at this time," I said.

He advised me that I would want to show good earnings once I offered the option. Nothing like stock purchases had ever been an issue through the early years when we were struggling to break even, but now I had to consider the best path to take.

My accountant explained to me that the difference between tax-oriented versus earnings-oriented companies, as I would soon learn, was the difference between long-range planning versus immediate gratification. It meant I would suppress my earnings in order to minimize my taxes. I would do that by writing off *every* expense I could think of, without spreading my depreciation over a period of years. That way, I would reap the greatest personal benefit. A.J. Scribante, not MAJERS, would be the beneficiary of any future success, since we were a sub-chapter S-corporation at that time.

Because tax orientation does not focus on retained earnings, chances were MAJERS would remain small if I went the tax-orientation route, which is designed to deliver the best life for the company's owner, but not necessarily the company. It limits the business's growth and, in essence, denies a partnership with Uncle Sam.

Earnings orientation meant growth orientation to me. With earnings orientation, I would start to defer payments by *depreciating* rather than deducting, for instance, a new piece of office equipment in the year of purchase. I would depreciate it over the next five years to protect our earnings stream.

"When you show greater earnings you pay more taxes—to your partner, Uncle Sam," my accountant told me. "But the retained earnings *after* taxes will be returned to the business as retained capital, and now the business has a base from which to grow. Over time, you become more growth-oriented, and, in due time, you can take the company public if you wish. Naturally, companies still must *minimize* their tax payments, even in an earnings-oriented firm, so you have to work through that. After all, you don't want Uncle Sam to become the managing partner." He leaned back and smiled.

"Only a few companies can generate enough capital to finance their own growth," he said.

I took his advice, depreciating instead of deducting, focusing on the future of the company instead of the temporary comfort of the boss. Growth was important to me, and MAJERS, so I took MAJERS the growth route for tax purposes by taking Uncle Sam on as my partner. At the time we were able to set aside a portion of our profits for the company's profit-sharing program. MAJERS consistently showed increasing internal stock value, gaining an impressive 50 percent a year in the earlier years and close to 40 percent annually during our later years. Earnings orientation paid off handsomely for MAJERS. When we occupied the second floor office in the old WOW Building, we couldn't afford to have carpet on the wooden floor. Over time, because we put aside some of our earnings, we were able to carpet the floor and buy new equipment.

Ultimately our eyes were on growth and the value of our stock. MAJERS was able to provide the creature comforts for all of us, executives and employees alike, and still show impressive earnings. In 1972, I informed the original two directors, "You have the opportunity to buy stock in the company at fifty cents per share." They agreed. The next step was to have the company stock valued each year by an independent investment banker, Bob Kathol of Kirkpatrick, Pettis, Smith, and Polian. "We will evaluate the company based on your financial growth and your earnings performance," Bob said. "Because you are a private company, we are going to use a more conservative evaluation than is the standard in the industry, but it should be more consistent."

The stock showed a nice gain and the value of earnings became apparent. It served as a great motivator for the employees to always focus on efficiency of operation.

■ ■ ■

The world's best planning for a small company could never have forecasted what happened to MAJERS in the early 1970s. When the OPEC oil price increased in 1973 and 1974, our business exploded. The price of plastic containers increased and all hydrocarbon products increased as did many other aspects of the economy.

The CPG companies wanted to get out of the promotion expenditure business since they couldn't evaluate its effectiveness. They offered grocery chains and the wholesalers buying allowances ahead of the product price increase. The wholesalers bought everything they could since they made great margin on the other side of price increases by not bringing the prices down so quickly when they fell.

In September of 1974, the wholesalers and chains stopped buying product because they had filled their warehouses to the brim by saving 10 percent on purchases. It finally dawned on them that interest was approaching 16 percent to carry the inventory.

That's when we got a big break. Without promotional funds from major brands, the retailers began featuring private label brands. They quickly learned that they could be effective in moving product through their weekend features and displays. Consumers were more apt to buy private-label products because they were often substantially cheaper than name brands. Private-label tuna went from an eight-share of the market to a twelve-share—not good news for the Starkist and Chicken of the Sea people.

Typically, by November of each year, the Vlasic pickle company would move their entire inventory to the market. But in November of 1975 they still had inventory on hand. Vlasic had to find a way to keep moving their products off shelves. Companies like theirs wondered what to do, and an answer soon became clear: "Let's pump some promotional money into the market and move the inventory!"

We were at the right place at the right time. Promotional dollars began flooding into the market. As the expenditures grew, the focus was directed to MAJERS to provide the measurement and information so vastly needed. Our growth was developing, and we were on our way.

■ ■ ■

One day, Frank Schanne came to me and asked, "What would you do if Lever Brothers informed us that they were eliminating our $540,000 contract?"

"I would get on the phone immediately and call Tom Carroll," I said.

Frank and I had first met Tom Carroll at an SMI luncheon meeting where he was the featured speaker. So when we called him at Lever Brothers, the global manufacturing company, he knew of MAJERS and, more importantly, he knew Frank Schanne and me. We were able to make an appointment with him.

"We should create a sense of urgency and tell him that it is important and that we'd like to see him tomorrow," I told Frank.

But Tom didn't bite—for a very good reason. "Gee, as much as I'd be willing to see you guys tomorrow, I can't. I just had my staff meeting and one of my executive VPs fell over dead in my office and we've been very busy just getting all of that taken care of," he said. "I answered the phone thinking it was the ambulance."

He saw us soon after.

Frank and I knew Tom Carroll needed MAJERS help. He was the CEO of Lever Brothers in a year when the company lost $12 million. Frank Schanne made a presentation to executives at Lever Brothers, including Tom Carroll, demonstrating the penny margin of difference between Coke and Pepsi featured by the retailer, Pepsi having the lower price. He then showed how there was a ten-cent difference between Era and Wisk detergents. Wisk was the leading share brand and received the lower price, and Wisk moved about 240 million total units annually, half of which moved on promotion, would be 120 million units. Frank showed Lever Brothers how, at a ten-cent margin, this lower price differential explained the $12 million that Lever Brothers lost that year.

Also, the retailers we had interviewed told us that Lever Brothers was always *last* to present their promotional offers to stores. Since Era was already featured and the consumer shelves were full, it demanded a lower price for the last-in brand. Timing was both the issue and the solution. Through good implementation of the MAJERS system, the lost revenue could have been saved on just one product alone.

Unfortunately, Tom Carroll did not have a chance to implement our program, which he saw as an opportunity to better his company. Lever Brothers out of London introduced a new CEO, an Englishman, and we were not able to get the new British CEO up to speed in time in terms of the promotional process. Win some, lose some.

■ ■ ■

Quaker Oats hot cereal was being moved from Best Food Day (Wednesday or Thursday) to Early Week in retail grocery ads across the U.S. because of their dominant share of the marketplace. Quaker Oats had demanded that we report all features as just a total rather than breaking them out by Best Food Day and Early Week (Monday or Tuesday) features.

Retailers used Quaker's products and their promotional offers to build their early week traffic in the stores through the checkouts. They found that by running Quaker Oats on a Sunday, Monday, or Tuesday, that they could entice the customers in during the back-to-school and winter months with the Hot Quaker Oats and the instant Quaker Oats. They would then run the competitive brand of hot oats on Best Food Day. This way, the retailer would build their early week traffic and would still have a hot cereal promotion for the Best Food Day or weekend sale.

As a result, Quaker Oats was losing share of market and was not maintaining their sales during that key sales period. Our data and our analysis showed them what was happening. As a result, they shifted their program, and the next year on their September back-to-school hot cereal promotion they told this story to the retail trade based upon the findings that we had presented to them. Quaker focused on getting the Best Food Day ads as reported by MAJERS and getting A features.

Naturally, the retailers wanted to cooperate with Quaker. The retailer's request of any manufacturer at the outset of distribution of any of their products is simple: "Are you going to advertise it and are you going to build a brand franchise?"

Naturally, after that franchise is built the last thing the retailer should want to do would be to erode it since it is to his advantage to have strong national brands to support. That year Quaker received more A features and their program was the most successful that they had ever had. They put some contests around the greatest achievement and focused in on getting features, making it their greatest profit contribution year yet. That promotion alone generated several million dollars to the Quaker Oats corporate profit in hot cereals.

During the 1973–1974 period we helped another client, Heinz, increase its share from 20 percent up to 42 percent, partially through the use of A feature activity, and partially through improvements in their technology of developing tomato paste.

Because of the fluctuation in the crop, tomatoes would be great one year and then not so great the next year. Therefore, the ability to promote tomatoes relied more upon the weather than it did upon the marketing plan. Heinz found a way around this by storing tomato paste through refrigeration technology. They were able to sustain the program against a marketing plan and really take the market away from their competitors—at that time, Hunt's, Del Monte, and Schneider.

Heinz always had product in a down crop market and therefore could promote ketchup when others didn't have the inventory. The retailers were happy and so were Heinz and MAJERS. We made a great team.

■ ■ ■

Later, another exciting development for MAJERS would be the move to online access for clients. At any time, online clients with their own computer terminals could network into the MAJERS system and request and retrieve information that otherwise would come to them more slowly in the form of a printed report. The number of online clients was growing each day, and the first two in 1975 were Hunt Foods and Coca-Cola. The ability to enter data directly into the computer would be a boon to MAJERS media analysts too.

What began in 1963 as a one-man study of newspaper ads had grown into a highly sophisticated service for American businesses. Over five hundred employees worked for us, each a specialist in his own field.

Later, we set up an online computer hook up so that Hunt Foods in Fullerton, California, could receive information directly from our database in Omaha. Dale Hardner, their marketing executive, came to check out the system. "You have done this in record time. How many people were on the project team?"

"Only Ray Johnson and I, with some minor assistance from others," Red Byars told him.

"If Hunt Foods would have done this it would have taken a project leader, a couple of EDP systems experts, some programmers . . . possibly ten or so on the team and better than six months work," said Hardner. "Your guys did it in two months."

Things were looking up, especially when IBM, a company I'd long admired, invited me for a visit. In 1974 the district manager for IBM, George Archer, invited me to a planning session with IBM in Atlanta—and didn't ask me to make my own way to the company headquarters. "We will fly you and someone else of your choice on the company plane to show you our planning process," Archer told me.

I had never been on a private plane, plus the visit would be thrilling and enlightening. We arrived at IBM in Atlanta, where we were shown a presentation of their growth rate, which was 15 percent, as well as their profit margin, which was 15 percent after tax, and their planning process, which stretched ten years into the future.

"We have a ten-year process which consists of two years of budgeted plans," one of the executives said. "For instance, our revenue is $40 billion, therefore next year we need $6 billion in new sales. Then the following year we'd like 15 percent of the $46 billion in order to maintain growth. The next five years our planning process involves focusing on the opportunities we have uncovered in the final three-year period. The process is ongoing."

I was astounded. "How do you achieve your earnings plan of 15 percent after tax?" I asked.

The company achieved it by having a "gross profit" before taxes and prior to some miscellaneous charges of 37 percent.

"If the new product or service won't allow that margin, it doesn't get out of the box," I was told.

The visit was an epiphany for me. I began to realize that as a company and as a management team we needed to know where we were going, not just where we had been. We needed to understand what lay beyond next week and next month. Budgets, financial stability, hiring practices, new products, sales quotas—these things had not been part of my business consciousness when MAJERS was small and mine alone. But now, things were different. We were embarking upon on a growth path of our own. Like IBM, potential clients were calling and asking us to set up a meeting to inform them of our service. I was determined to plan for the future so that we could expand MAJERS, its services, and its markets.

But we weren't like IBM. Not yet, anyway.

A major development that made me realize we were just reacting to the market came with the addition of data processing to our services. Did we plan for data processing? *No.* Did we lay out carefully organized reasons and methods for it? *No.* In the past, our clients' needs forced our short-range planning, as when Procter & Gamble suggested we computerize our data.

Now, other customers were getting more sophisticated in their need for information on their promotional expenditures. To begin planning the next step in our development, I put together budgets. I projected sales figures based on past performances: I gave more thought to the kinds of people we wanted to hire. When it became necessary to tell our employees what MAJERS's plans were, I'd be the one to let them know. I wasn't exactly running the company from my shirt pocket, but like the typical entrepreneur, orders flowed from my office. But we needed to do more than react to the market. We needed a solid long-range plan. As always, I waited, and, pretty soon, a messenger arrived to point me toward my future.

■ ■ ■

In 1974, my old friend Richard A. "Dick" Westcott dropped in to see me one day. We had just implemented the SRI evaluation system and were in our new offices.

Dick said he'd just resigned as president of Wheeler's, a chain of discount stores headquartered in Grand Island, Nebraska, and was soon to become CEO of a 7-Up bottling company in Des Moines.

"Dick, would you consider being a director for MAJERS?" I asked him.

"Let's have dinner next week and I'll think about it," he said.

For a long time we talked about how to best run a company. Dick apparently was good at it, and I was thrilled when he accepted my invitation to become a director. He suggested we see each other at least once a month to talk business. One of his first suggestions was that he meet each of our top six or eight managers. I loved the idea. That way, he could tell me what my managers were doing wrong. But instead of telling me what they were doing wrong, Dick told me what *I* was doing wrong.

"I suggest you get into the proper planning mode," he said.

"What do you mean?" I asked. "I've put together five-year and ten-year plans! I can put together a projection showing where the company is going and how we can reach our profit margin objectives! I have all of that laid out in great detail!"

"I'm not talking about what you're doing," he replied. "I'm talking about *involving* your people in the planning process. It's important to have them participate, so they can share ownership of the company's accomplishments."

I didn't hear him. Instead, I kept defending myself. I proudly showed him how meticulously I had calculated budgets, advising the data processing crew, for example, that they could spend $350,000. Data processing received a certain percentage of revenue, and if they needed more, the sales people had to bring in more revenue, because data processing was limited to this percentage of revenue.

I had devised this system all by myself; it wasn't something some outside consultant had calculated for me. I thought it worked pretty well. Based on past performance, I projected growth of 40 percent for the coming year. Again, I was pleased with the figures and that my system was working.

Dick stopped me in my tracks. "But nobody in your management team owns this," he said. "Only *you* own it. How do you propose to get *them* involved?"

He had me there.

He pulled out a slender volume from his briefcase, *Long-Range Planning for Your Business*, by Merritt L. Kastens, published by a division of the American Management Associations. It outlined the operations, the manipulations, and the actions that constitute a planning procedure.

"Most texts about planning tell you how to *think* about planning," he said. "This book tells you how to *do* it."

I read the book that evening, and then what Dick was telling me began to dawn on me from the book.

"Strategic planning is the mechanism for exercising leadership, and therefore it must be done by the people who expect to lead. It must begin with the CEO and involve the management team. Planning implies change. It's the companies that are operating in the most rapidly changing environments that do the best planning. They have to," the book stated.

It was only then that I realized the true value of a planning process done right. *Ownership*! I wouldn't be the only one to own the plan and have the responsibility to achieve the results. The team and, eventually, the entire organization would embrace and implement the plans, department by department.

The book affirmed that I was already doing a pretty good job, but as Dick pointed out, I was keeping it all to myself. So I took Dick's advice: I brought together eight of my managers to talk about long range planning for MAJERS. First, we devised our mission statement: "To help our clients better manage their promotional expenditures through the use of our information systems of the weekly newspaper advertising specials by grocery retailers."

Later, it would be revised to read: "Our mission is to be the BEST at providing information which will help our clients manage their marketing expenditures for competitive advantage."

Next, we began the process of including others in our planning sessions.

One of our VPs, Jim Vanderholm, called it his R-B-Do process. "Who are ('R') we, who do we want to be ('B'), and what do we need to do ('DO') to get there?"

The process is not complicated, especially if you do it in terms of the agenda.

Our first long-range planning meeting was with our six key managers. I set the agenda for the next six meetings to be held once a week, with two-hour sessions from 11 a.m. to 1 p.m. over lunch.

We began by defining who we were. Each member brought forth his or her own mission statement. From those six inputs we developed "Who we were." Then we listed and evaluated our strengths, weaknesses, and corporate assets. Much discussion time was invested. The process was in motion. Then we defined what we wanted to be, began developing strategies for each asset, and set goals for the year. From those monthly meetings our next year's plan evolved.

We then took the long-range planning technique throughout the company so each department could develop their own mission statement, in support of the corporate mission. What this did for the company was to provide a focus for our daily efforts, a sense of ownership and belonging, and a well-defined reason to show up on Monday.

Washington Post publisher and CEO Katherine Graham put it best when she said, "When you love what you do and you know that it matters, nothing could be more fun." When you know that it matters it means there is a worthwhile sense of purpose in what you do. You have a mission for your work. Just like a good schoolteacher, our military personnel, our nurses, and our doctors all know *why* they go to work.

At each company meeting I reinstated this credo: "Our mission is that the purpose is significant and you are critically important in its fulfillment every day."

The first year, 1974, we spent two weeks going through the corporation-wide planning process. Each manager was the expert in his department, but no manager was allowed to limit himself to just his field of expertise. The sales manager contributed to the financial plan, and the data processing manager suggested hiring procedures.

The mission stated the nature of our business. But there was more to it than that. We saw six assets as needing careful management: people, equipment, data, facilities, capital, and perhaps the most critical asset of all, our reputation.

Strategic planning is an ongoing process. We defined our assets in the initial sessions and as we continued the process the refinement brought forth requests. "We need great people and SRI is the way to access the talent," Frank Schanne said. "That must be a part of our policy."

"We must always have a state of the art computers and equipment in order to hire and retain great EDP talents," said Red Byars. "If you want to have rabbit stew, you must first catch the rabbit." I never could figure out what the rabbit was.

But one of the most important aspects of our planning process was pricing, and it was agreed to by all that we needed to set the price for our data relative to the value the client agreed to pay. As in any pricing process, we set our profit objective, and then it was up to the marketing manager to achieve that goal with their clients.

"A nice place to work is a great motivator and a part of the recognition process." I said.

Our profit would support our growth with acquisition, facilities, and equipment.

Next we needed policies, or guidelines, for controlling our assets. Here's what we devised as our most important missions:

People: We would recruit, hire, motivate, and retain the finest talents we could find.

Equipment: We would have state-of-the-art equipment. We would not sell information from outdated computers. We would pay top dollar to acquire state-of-the-art computers necessary to accommodate the latest in software development.

Data: This asset was the subject of considerable discussion, some of it for the first time. We had taken our data for granted and often treated it as a public matter, available to anyone who wanted it, and not as a kind of personal jewel box. We owned reams of information, and I learned that we shouldn't give information away any more than we should give capital away. *Nothing has a value until you give it a value.* If a client were buying information on flour, he might ask the sales rep for the national trend on shortening. The rep, eager to please, would tell the client. But the national trend on shortening was a piece of information we had worked hard to obtain, and we had to charge for it. If the customer agreed to the charge, then we knew the information was important to him. If he refused to pay, then we knew they didn't place much value on it.

Facilities: We wanted a nice, clean work place, as modern and comfortable as we could afford. Functional, nothing excessive, but something that motivated our employees and let them know we cared about them.

Capital: We would set a growth rate for ourselves based on past performance. We had been growing at the rate of about 50 percent a year, but we realized that rate might be unreasonable for the future. We adjusted it downward to 35 percent, which we still considered high enough to present a challenge. I wanted to push for 40 percent, before tax profit, but the closest we came was 37 percent before taxes.

Reputation: I don't know how many companies actually list "reputation" as an asset in their long-range planning, but we considered it our most important asset. We wanted to be reliable, honest, and honorable. As the saying goes, it takes a long time to build a good reputation, but only a short time to destroy it. We would always have to be careful that our actions were in tune with our reputation.

So much for our assets. We ended up as good planners as we completed the process by developing the strategies and goals for each asset. For example, the strategy for maintaining good people was to rely on the SRI process, varying it for the different positions as our selection tool. The rule became: if a manager didn't get an acceptable reading from the potential employee's SRI interview, the applicant was not hired.

■ ■ ■

Planning is evolutionary, not revolutionary.

One of our early clients said, "Don't become so flexible that you're limp or so firm that you become rigid. It's a delicate balance," he said, "As you think, think customer service.

We planned well for the future, but as we headed there we learned that there was always room for improvement. Once, one of our four members of the board of directors asked me: "What are your long-term measurements for the business?"

"We have two and three-year plans," I said. "That includes the budget."

"That's not what I'm asking you," he said. "What are your *long*-term measurements?"

"I can't answer that," I said. "Give me some time and I'll get back to you."

I spent several days talking to many people and came back with three measurements, which, when I think about it now, are valid for any company.

1) Return on Equity: How fast are we going to grow the company? What is our margin on sales? And how much debt are we willing to acquire? This measurement requires good sales and marketing as well as good financial management and forces you to think and plan on a longer than one year basis. It is a strategic measurement. Our return on equity chart showed the relationship of the three key elements: asset turnover (growth), margin on sales, and debt to equity. The trend in the 1982 chart showed the return on equity at 39.8 percent in 1981 and 39.1 percent in 1982.

2) Employee Retention: Employee retention requires good executive management. If you provide employees with a decent work environment, treat them with

respect, and don't exploit them, then compensation becomes just one of several reasons to stay. Good recognition requires good planning, and retention is a function of good management. Each year we conducted employee surveys to know where we needed to change and improve.

3) Client Retention: The information business is not an easy business. It regularly requires consistent timelines, accuracy, and value. We decided our canceled business would not exceed 7 percent. This figure told us whether or not our client service was working and how well we were managing people. Some clients would fall by the wayside as their needs changed, but we never wanted them to cancel our service because we weren't doing our job. Our field managers knew we were watching this closely, and they responded. We would tolerate deviations from the company's way of doing things, but we wouldn't tolerate poor results.

Taken over the long haul, these three measurements give a clear picture of how the company is performing—and the MAJERS board agreed saying, "Keep up the great work. Those numbers are tremendous."

■ ■ ■

The strategic planning and long-term measurements process worked well until about 1982, but by the mid-1980s we needed to refine our financial long-term planning. We had continued to grow without a CFO, and we needed financial discipline in our planning meetings. The board encouraged the hiring of a finance person with an economic and an accounting background. I set out to find the right person and, almost immediately, one name stood above all the rest: Joe Konen. Joe became vice president for finance at MAJERS. He interpreted and translated financial data into actionable information. Joe had a great reference: "Dr. Death," SRI's Jim Sorensen. He knew that Joe Konen had an extensive background in economics and was leaving his current position. He'd worked for General Foods, and was experienced in mergers and acquisitions.

MAJERS was profitable, but nobody was asking, "How profitable should we be?" We began to turn our attention to how to increase the value of our stockholders' shares in the company. We had some guidelines about meeting customers' needs, but we didn't have much about trying to have the performance of the company meet the stockholders' needs.

He showed us how the budget translates into the performance of the stock and what action the company needed to improve the value of the stock. In his first meeting with the executive team, Joe pointed out that our mission was marketing-focused and not financially represented. "Let me show you what I mean," Joe said.

He put up the slide showing how we could continue to grow, with a greater emphasis on the financial elements and our share of the research information market. "One point that is apparent: you have allowed the administration costs to reach 11 percent," Joe said. "This should be reduced by at least three points. Marketing costs should be studied, along with the pricing of our products. The margin on sales needs to be improved by looking at the profit performance of the client. All of this will help to improve the stockholder value."

While not everything occurred according to plan, we learned that the process of planning was invaluable. We also learned also that a specific blueprint is the *only* way to direct energy and evaluate results. We weren't always on target, but were usually on course, and strategic long-range planning dramatically replaced the seat-of-the-pants approach.

By 1972, my personal plan was to have an employee stock ownership program in effect within the year. At that time, the board authorized five million shares for sale. I set up the "A" value voting stock that was held entirely by me. The directors and the employees were sold the "B" stock, which was also occasionally contributed to the profit-sharing plan.

With profit sharing and stock ownership, my dream to share the benefits of hard work and dedication with the employees was now becoming a reality.

THE SHELF OF

Growth

Early on, I had a friend who headed a large advertising and public relations agency that, at the time, was much larger than MAJERS. I figured I could pick his brain about how to run a business. Both of us provided a service to our clients, and creativity was the basis of both our services.

He knew I wanted to grow my business, just as he had grown his, and in the course of our conversation he told me something I never forgot: "As you grow, you must decide whether you want to be big or good. You can't be both."

Naturally, I wanted MAJERS be good; we already were good and intended to stay that way as we expanded. But I also wanted to be big. As I discussed in the last chapter, growth was our plan. I knew that with experience and good people, we could provide new services for our clients, ask for bigger fees, and be one of the biggest and best in the information field.

Big or good? Big or good? The words kept repeating themselves in my brain. Why couldn't we be both? All night long in bed and into the dawn, I kept arguing his premise with my myself.

His remark, delivered so matter-of-factly, made me even more determined to remain good as we got bigger. As I think back on it, I suppose I should have thanked him, because from that day forward, his words were a constant reminder to me that as we got bigger we also had to remain true to our mission. To also not only be good, but to become great. Isn't that the mission of all great companies?

I considered the companies we served. Procter & Gamble was big, but it was also good. IBM, our supplier, was big and good. Perhaps Lever Brothers was a company my friend was referring to—big, but its profits weren't good. But the P&Gs and the IBMs of the world? They were both big and good—and that's what I was determined would be my company's destiny.

Growing bigger while maintaining our reputation for quality did pose major challenges for us. One of those was in employee retention, especially among our younger employees. When we were a smaller company, we were able to hire quality young people, but we didn't grow rapidly enough to give them the added responsibility they wanted. They sought challenge and the opportunity to move up the company ladder—more money, more authority, more chances to test their abilities. But we couldn't provide these all at once. We promoted from within whenever possible, although we weren't reluctant to go outside. But as a company grows, its employees expect promotions to be from within.

We refused to grow haphazardly, and this problem of employee retention, especially among our young employees, became a problem. As our markets expanded, we tried to give employees a sense of ownership by developing new services that they could both foster and grow.

Soon, we outgrew our home office space. We occupied the second floor of a pet products company with four thousand square feet, where Red Byars parked his old car in the #1 parking stall every day. We remained there four years. In 1976 we moved to southwest Omaha into a building with ten thousand square feet. Eighteen months later we added another ten thousand square feet. Then our landlord ran into financial difficulties and couldn't pay for the additional space we quickly needed, so we bought his building and, in 1980, expanded it to forty-two thousand square feet.

Still, that wasn't enough. We bought fifteen acres of land across the street from our building and constructed a new two-story headquarters of forty-thousand square feet. It had wings stretching from the main building, which were connected with an overhead walkway to the older buildings. Completed in 1984, this gave us a total of eighty-two thousand square feet. By then, we were most certainly big— the good part would require constant vigilance to maintain.

■ ■ ■

MAJERS began as a collector of information. Our first phase was data gathering, collating, key punching, manipulating, and storing in a way that would allow us to fulfill our customers' needs. The second phase was data processing. That's where we standardized our forms and systems for processing, which were, of course, dictated by our growth.

The next stage was data interpretation. In order to do good work in this phase we needed experienced professional people who were familiar with our customers and the way we applied information. We needed people who were able to both sell the product and service our customers. These two elements were essential if we were to continue to grow and be good.

Our final stage was that of data intelligence. This is where we combined our experience, knowledge, and production ability with the professional talents of our client service departments and made recommendations for the application of our information to help our customers better manage their promotional expenditures.

As we entered the final stage, a significant factor in our continued growth was the hiring of Frank Schanne as sales manager. He came to MAJERS in 1975, and would eventually become our executive VP and COO. Frank had strong growth orientation and was a superb recruiter. With our system for selection, he brought into the company people who gave us exceptional development. Someone once said, "gross profits come from sales and net profits come from management." Thanks to Frank, our sales people gave us both.

Frank Schanne's first hire was Warren Archer, product manager for the Nestle's Quick Brand. Warren made his revenue plan each year. Then others joined. Bill Wyman, Larry White, Dick Schaefer, John O'Keefe, Rich Olson, David House, Mike Allen—all of whom became vice presidents with revenue and management responsibilities.

Frank's skills and the talented individuals he brought to MAJERS propelled us with dynamic growth over the next several years. From the late seventies forward,

we grew at the rate of 35 percent per year, compounded annually for fifteen con-
secutive years. At the same time we grew the profit margin by two to three points
each year. My goal had been 40 percent before tax profit—but our internal stock
value grew at the rate of 50 percent per year.

Frank often said, "We have made a commitment to each other and to our customers, and we haven't failed either one!" He made sure we were big and good—
and never fell into the cursed stage of bureaucracy, allowing his sales people full
reign.

A good illustration of this was when David House, who handled the Mrs. Paul's
Frozen Food account, was making a presentation of our information to the vice
presidents and senior sales people in the audience. The CEO of Paul's joined the
audience a few minutes after the presentation started. David is a tremendous talent, and did a great job. Upon completion, the CEO approached him and said,
"David, that was the finest, most informative sharing of key information we have
ever had at this company. But why didn't I get a presentation booklet?"

David replied, "Sir, we took a vote before you came in and the group agreed not
to give you one because you wouldn't understand it."

The company's executives' mouths dropped. But the CEO broke out in a big
laugh. David's ego, courage, and sense of humor won over the company that day.

In 1983 we created our SUMMA Group in response to the needs of manufacturers and retailers for analysis of the often-bewildering abundance of raw marketing material we provided them.

Not long after that, we embarked on an ambitious program of expansion aimed
at bringing all our data together in a way that would capture a major share of the
market for promotional information services. The goal: to provide the few additional services we weren't already offering.

We also sought out synergistic companies to acquire. We were already collecting information on supermarket displays and featured items as well as coupons, all
of which helped our clients increase their share of the market. For the display information, we contracted with a company called RGIS, which stood for Retail Grocery Inventory Service.

RGIS was a small company owned by two brothers who had created a culture
similar to ours. Their people were hard workers who did stock inventories for a single supermarket or an entire chain. It became obvious that while counting cans and

boxes, bags and bottles, fruits and vegetables, they were also able to inventory the special displays in a store for MAJERS's data collection. Since they already were in the supermarket, their work for us didn't entail much extra effort, and it was invaluable.

Then we found another small firm called TRIM, which collected information from checkout counters. Checkout scanners are those devices that "beep" as an item is passed over an electronic slot. Today, the fancier ones boast an electronic voice that announces the price out loud. Scanners provide the supermarket manager with instant and precise information on the number of units of any product sold. Scanner information tells the manager when to restock shelves and when to place orders with suppliers.

We now had enough different ways of collecting data to give each client instant information as to how his promotional dollars were performing. The supermarket customer is the ultimate judge of that effectiveness, and we could tell our client immediately how the consumer was spending his or her grocery dollars.

We were big and getting bigger—all the while remaining true to our mission of also being good.

THE SHELF OF

Structuring Models

“**O**nly a fool learns from his own mistakes. A wise man learns from the mistakes of others.”—Otto Von Bismarck

Although my first association with IBM was a troublesome one for MAJERS because of the glitches we encountered computerizing our data, I nonetheless consider IBM one of the best-run companies in America—alongside Procter & Gamble. I regarded these companies so highly that we patterned many aspects of MAJERS's professional corporate structure after them.

I have two corporate histories on my office bookshelf. One is *Eyes on Tomorrow: The Evolution of Procter & Gamble*, by Oscar Schisgall, and the other is *IBM: Colossus in Transition*, by Robert Sobel. I've learned much from both books. Both IBM and P&G are far bigger than MAJERS Corporation ever hoped to be, but the wise and innovative decisions made through the years by their executives can be applied to almost any business.

In 1974 we were struggling with the typed contracts we developed. They were what are called "evergreen" contracts, and required a six-month notice to cancel or they were automatically renewed for another year.

Almost every time we submitted them they were passed to the legal department for review and approval. But instead of getting automatically approved, the contract became, in many cases, a point of contention; a great opportunity for younger corporate attorneys to cut their teeth. They changed the jurisdiction from Nebraska to where the contracts were located, modified the notice, which forced us to go and defend them to uphold the conditions. So much time was wasted!

One day in 1974, I was at my desk and Red Byars came in with an IBM representative and an IBM lease contract. The IBM contract was printed on three-ply paper, but was only one page. Our contracts were two pages because our typeface was so large. I immediately liked the IBM contract better. "If I wanted to modify one of these conditions, how would I do it?" I asked the IBM rep.

"You wouldn't," he replied. "And if you tried I couldn't give you the lease. That contract is set in stone."

Aha! We had just solved our contract challenge. I told my assistant, Ann Rosenthal, "Call the printer and have our contract put on one page! White paper! Fine type! And make it a three-ply document!"

We adopted IBM's three-part printed contract format which was simple and easy to understand. This gave an appearance of simplicity, as well as permanence, and seemed to calm the customer's fears that he had to have it rewritten by his attorney. He might change a word or two and add a few commas, but the old business of rewriting the entire contract came to a stop.

The new contracts were simpler and more concise, and, like IBM, set in stone—which gave us a more professional appearance and lessened our time with our client's lawyers, freeing us to concentrate on our quality service.

I don't especially like the word "copy." Emulate might be a better term. We weren't above emulating successful methods from other successful companies and molding them to fit our needs. We only emulated methods, not specifics, and we never emulated other marketing research companies. We didn't have to do that. We were unique and a pioneer in our industry, much the same was IBM did when they pioneered the computer.

We emulated even the giants—IBM and P&G—every chance we got. First, in attitude and style. I greatly admired IBM's aggressiveness in the marketplace. They were always pushing the ball uphill. They didn't react to changes, they *created* them.

They forced the marketplace to move in a certain direction with new products and the finest sales talent they could find.

We did the same thing in the same way—with the finest sales talent we could find and by creating products that revolutionized our industry, just as IBM's products (the computer, the electric typewriter, disc storage units, etc.) revolutionized its industry.

I knew a lot about IBM. By 1975, I had gathered twenty years of IBM's financial statistics and studied them closely, trending their figures. You could see their return on equity, their gross margins, and their margin on sales. They set their growth rate at 15 percent a year and never failed in that goal during those years.

The same with their margin on sales—a straight 37 percent before tax. The same with debt to equity—another straight line for twenty years. I'd always looked at IBM figures and figured they did it automatically, through great products and great service. But after studying the data, I discovered it was much more than that on a sales trip to IBM's Atlanta office. I learned of IBM's planning process. Their managers told me they set up the objectives and then worked like crazy to achieve them. Managers have to manage against those goals, they said.

They are also realistic. When IBM brings out a new product, the product is expected to achieve 37 percent margin on sales. The older products have to take up the slack. I immediately decided I'd emulate that system for the new products we introduced. All of our special reports were priced at a 40 percent margin before tax.

Although by 1974, IBM manufactured a variety of products, its management viewed the company as primarily a service company. MAJERS, too, was a service company, which is why I found it profitable to study IBM's methods. IBM's focus was always on customer service and their highest-priced margin allowed them to provide a quality of service that was unmatched. It's closest then-competitor, NCR, with its lower margin, just couldn't compete.

■ ■ ■

Just as IBM's success sparked a slew of would-be competitors, the emulators began circling MAJERS.

When we started MAJERS, our service was unique and we had no head-to-head competitors. But a few years later a company called Advertising Checking Bureau surfaced, which provided packaged goods manufacturers with newspaper advertising tear sheets and tried to move into our field of analyzing and trending supermarket promotion.

When I called on Starkist Tuna for the first time, my contact said, "We are using ACB, but I like your approach much better."

After getting the order, I asked the Starkist man, "What does ACB do and what did they do for you?"

He pulled out a manually typed report showing the retail space in "lineage," a term used in the administrative world to denote size and not dominance. This was reported by brand and by market and retailer. It was a very basic report and very cheaply priced. I encountered two other users in my selling effort and also replaced their ACB reports. At this time it was a sideline for them, much the same as "Brand Action" was, but ACB was not a company that we were interested in.

By this time, we were providing this information by computer, and ACB was still doing it by hand, with most of their information coming out of their home base of New York City and controlled by their managers in that city. In 1974 during the recession, advertising was starting to wane and promotion was growing. ACB's business was falling off; and they moved into the promotional field by reporting lineage only.

We met the challenge by becoming even more aggressive in our sales and customer service approaches. ACB gave us a little grief by trying to compete on the basis of lower prices and data only. There was no customer service whatsoever. They never took any business from us but they did land some minor contracts from smaller, unsophisticated users. I had always admired the way IBM looked after its customers, and I emulated that approach for MAJERS.

From my observation, IBM's competitive strategy was to compete with *themselves* by bringing out faster and better computer systems every two or three years. By the time the competition was in a position to match equipment, IBM moved to the next higher level of technology. First was the 1401 model computer, then the 1440, after which came the 360 with several improved models and then the 4143s came next and so forth. The competition couldn't afford to compete.

In my quest to stay ahead of the competition, I often turned to Tom Wilson, Senior Partner of McKinsey in New York. At one of our twice-a-year meetings, he asked me, "How has technology helped the MAJERS Corporation of the past few years?"

Searching for an answer, I had asked Neal Greenberg to do a study to determine the impact. After four months of search and development, Neal's study determined that we had realized about a 6 percent advantage in our operation expense to sales. We could show charts that would demonstrate this point. What the study also pointed out: as a result of the talent, experience, and the power of our sales organization, we were able to increase our prices in the range of 20–25 percent in some cases.

As a result of the sales performance and the increase in our revenue due to pricing, we were improperly reflecting an efficiency that we felt we were getting in the area of production. We felt that the production was making great contributions to our overall profit margin improvement, whereas it was actually the sales organization that was bringing about the greatest efficiency, through pricing, and the contribution that production was making was providing an exceptionally accurate and fine product for the marketplace.

While we were showing corporations how to beat their competitors, we were also doing our best to stay ahead of our own.

Our information was 99.95 percent accurate. But it was sometimes being compared with competitors that, in some cases, were using 80 percent accurate data at a price that was about one-third of our price. A director of market research from one of our clients visited our Omaha operation. After the tour of our facility, he said, "I am highly impressed with the technology that you employ in gathering the information that you provide to your clients, and I am also highly impressed with the attitude of the people as I observed them doing their work. They are happy, they are dedicated, they are knowledgeable, and they are sincere in their efforts to perform and produce the finest."

I was certainty glad to hear that. "Did you by chance observe the effort that we go through to insure the accuracy of our information, to provide you with 99.95 percent accurate data?" I asked.

He said he did.

I informed him that the difference between data that is about 80 percent accurate and that which 99.95 percent is accurate, that additional 19.5 percent accuracy better than doubles the initial base cost to deliver 80 percent accurate data. Quality costs money to produce. "And add on top of that the professionalism, knowledge of the client service people, individuals that give the data meaning and direction and help you to better manage your promotional expenditure. You then have our pricing structure."

For the first time he understood the pricing value of accurate information in our area. He also understood why our price was justified—especially when employing this system with a sales organization that is being evaluated on the basis of their ability to obtain features and displays.

■ ■ ■

Another feature of IBM business techniques that I emulated was their letter of intent, which they used in computer sales. Buying a computer is a major expense, and no businessperson enters that kind of agreement without considerable thought and comparison shopping. But there comes a moment when a decision must be made, and IBM's letter of intent nudges the shopper to decide on their product.

There is absolutely nothing binding about a letter of intent—which of course, merely states in a single paragraph, or two at most, that the customer intends to buy an IBM computer. The customer can back out any time they want, up to the final signing of the purchase contract. But once a customer signs the letter, about 90 percent of the decision is done. Rarely do they back out. Actually, the client usually becomes a supporter of the IBM machine, just as an auto buyer becomes a supporter of the model he purchases.

With its letter of intent, IBM could get production rolling back at its manufacturing plant, and when the computer was installed the final contract was signed. This way IBM was able to control its inventory and didn't have to store thousands of computers in its warehouses when business slowed. This practice protected IBM's unpublished policy for full employment and eliminated the need to lay off workers.

It was the perfect way to spur growth at MAJERS. Here's how we expressed our reasoning to the prospective client: "By signing this brief letter of intent, we can shorten the computer set-up time for your service. It is not a legal document. I'll bring you the actual contract as soon as we can define your service needs."

I adapted IBM's letter of intent idea and used it for our new customers, as well as when we were trying to sell new services to regular customers. We asked them to sign the letter while we worked out our program for them. Once the program was in place, we asked them to sign the formal contract. It was another step in becoming a more professionally run company.

I had several friends who worked for IBM in the Omaha district office and one of them told me Tom Watson's philosophy of compensation: pay a small base salary and a large commission on sales with no car allowance. The sales rep was allowed to make enough money to afford the car of their choice. Basic travel expenses were covered, and that was it. IBM hired the college graduates and trained them in the ways of IBM.

We were in a different situation. I felt we had to hire experienced individuals who were not in a position to start low with a high commission. They were married, usually with a family, so it wouldn't work quite the same way. But we did pay an appropriate base with a motivating commission plus an annual bonus for achieving their growth plan.

Another thing I emulated from IBM, with a little alteration to suit our particular needs, was their sales philosophy. They paid a low base salary and a very high commission. I decided on a slightly higher base salary, enough to pay a competitive salary, but I retained the high commission. We also paid commissions on positive net sales—another benefit derived from my insight into the IBM program. If the salesperson lost a contract account then they were required to make up the loss without commission. With MAJERS, their base of business justified their base salary and commissions were paid for growth of their territory. Our base salary represented approximately 55 percent of total compensation. Forty five percent was incentive.

A high commission gives sales people an opportunity to put their talents to work and earn more. Our SRI profiles showed us that people with excellent sales ability also typically have a lot of ego and courage. They enjoy the challenge of making it *big*. But it is important to reward them quickly. Pay the commission within a week, if possible, certainly by the end of the month. The commission check is a form of recognition, a pat on the back, an instant motivator for more. We always made an issue of handing over that check, quickly and enthusiastically. It was management's way of saying, *You've done a good job, and the closer you can get recognition to performance, the better off the company will be.*

Management personnel have their own perks, so they can wait until the end of the year for their special recognition and bonuses. But a year is too long to make salespeople wait.

Another thing I admired about IBM was that they worked hard to avoid becoming a bureaucracy. From everything I read, IBM seems to give its people a fair amount of freedom.

Tom Watson employed an open-door policy. Employees and even clients could gain access in times of need. The same policy worked well for MAJERS. Politics is a cancer in any business. It's nearly impossible not to have it in a company as it grows, but it is important to minimize it, to control it and, hopefully, eradicate it.

■ ■ ■

In his book, *In Search of Excellence*, Tom Peters uses the term "chunking" to describe the process of breaking down a company into chunks, or separate divisions or companies. Through my research, I discovered that IBM had "chunked" down into its computer division, its copier division, its typewriter division, and its supplies division, with a separate president for each.

We "chunked" down our field offices, where each vice president in charge was given considerable autonomy to operate within our general guidelines. We didn't try to "over-authoritize" the field vice president. We had methods and procedures, but the vice president didn't have to use those methods and procedures as long as our profit and customer service objectives were met.

IBM requires its salespeople to know the names of the chief executive officers of the companies they serve. In my case, whenever IBM transferred a new man or woman to Omaha, that person would soon be at my door just to say hello and express their appreciation for our business—a very nice touch. We emulated this system and paid a $500 incentive to those who did it.

As a result, if one of our clients decided to cut back on our services, usually a decision made by some vice president, our salesperson could gain access to the CEO's office to argue our case; it's the CEO who can influence a final decision.

I haven't discussed Procter & Gamble as much as IBM, but I have great admiration for them, too. Let's consider the differences and similarities of the two companies, using IBM's computer division for comparison.

IBM sells its computers to a variety of different industries—banks, insurance companies, wholesalers, retailers, hospitals, doctors, lawyers, universities, grade schools. Name an industry, and IBM will provide its computers. The computer division has one product and "dozens of knowledges"—those specialized bits of information you must learn about specific clients and their industries. They train their people to talk not just computer language, but also the language of the industry *buying* the computer.

P&G is just the opposite. P&G has dozens of products and one "knowledge"— how to sell their diverse products, whether it's Jiffy peanut butter, Crest toothpaste, Folgers coffee, or Duncan Hines cake mixes. Using the advertising media, they sell consumer packaged goods through the retailer to the customer. They know that responsibility very well. They take one knowledge and apply it to each product. Mr. Whipple sells Charmin tissue. Mrs. Olson sells Folgers coffee.

IBM and P&G are opposites in their methods, but similar in their successes.

MAJERS didn't have to emulate IBM's techniques of selling to diverse industries, because we sold our service to the packaged goods industry and we knew that industry as well as our customers. What we did was to hire brand managers who also had sales experience, and sales people from the various different companies within the CPG industry. Combined with the knowledge of a few market research and advertising individuals, the team of experts brought forth customer service programs to meet the market needs.

MAJERS was unique, but MAJERS was wise enough to learn from others. We never felt we needed to reinvent the wheel, unless there was no wheel to fit our vehicle.

■ ■ ■

However, I'd soon be looking beyond IBM and P&G toward other corporate giants. This time, we wouldn't be emulating: we'd be working with them as clients. We were on a roll, racking up as many new accounts as possible. I met with Lever Brothers on Park Avenue in New York and made a presentation to their brand and sales people, about ten individuals. I always began by introducing MAJERS, mentioning how we were headquartered in Omaha, Nebraska.

"If I were you, I wouldn't make a big deal about that!" someone interrupted.

It brought the house down and broke the ice. I didn't get the order then, but a few months and many calls later, I was in business with Lever Brothers, thanks to Dick Leuking, the marketing manager.

We landed General Mills, which was a great client to work with. They had wonderful, competent people and they used and respected our information extremely well. Their flour division improved the profitability of their product through better timing and promotional programs using MAJERS. We landed Land O' Lakes, which loved our information as well as our company.

Quaker Oats in Chicago was doing $200,000 in contract business with us when I received a call to cancel the business. They didn't implement the information because their market research personnel did not see its value. We lost the contract, but I decided not to wait for the cancellation, but instead to react ahead of it.

I assembled several special reports, one on hot and cold cereals, and others covering the categories we were selling to Quaker on a contract basis. I sold them as "specials" to Quaker, Post division of General Foods, and General Mills. At the end of the year I had sold $200,000 of specials to Quaker and copies of the same reports to others for an additional $100,000.

"When one door closes, another one opens," goes the chestnut phrase of philosophy. It is with that philosophy that I have always approached my life and my business. Everyone faces setbacks, but those who succeed never stop looking for new opportunities. It's the only way to grow.

■ ■ ■

As I mentioned, we were on a roll in the late seventies, and I was so focused on our burgeoning business that I honestly had little time to check my personal bank account. Then, I got a call that showed me how well we were doing.

"After reading the various articles in the newspaper about the growth and progress of MAJERS, it's become apparent to me that you need to think about expanding your coverage for tax purposes."

It was 1975, and Bob Billig, an acquaintance in the insurance business, was telling me something I really didn't know: "Do you realize what your net worth is?"

I honestly did not. My lifestyle was extremely comfortable, my family had everything we needed, and I was happy.

"How much profit will your company make this year?" he asked.

"Just short of a million," I said.

"If that's the case, at a low multiple of ten times earnings, your company is worth $10 million," he said. "At fifteen times earnings, it's worth $15 million."

It was the first time I realized that I had achieved my original goal. Yet, I also realized that my original goal in business—to make a lot of money—had been eclipsed by the mission of MAJERS.

THE SHELF OF

Perpetual Learning

This is the story of an organization and an individual who recognized the value of what MAJERS did, and by intelligently implementing that service and information, achieved great things for that organization. The company I am referring to is Pepsi, and the individual is the company's then vice president Bob Sander.

"Pepsi Takes on the Champ," read the cover story of the June 12, 1978, issue of *Business Week*. It could have read, "Bob Sander of Pepsi Takes On the Champ."

I had been working with Coca-Cola with ten markets of coverage and Pepsi Cola with three markets. Each one quickly expanded to our fifty-five market coverage, and then to our total 102 markets. Coca-Cola had been a client of MAJERS since the early days of our business, and they too recognized the value of the information we provided. Over the years their account with us grew significantly, and top management was always interested in our presentations.

All our accounts in the soft drink business received the same information. Coke was handled by our Atlanta office and Pepsi by our Stanford, Connecticut, office.

In our Chicago office we handled RC while the Omaha office handled Dr. Pepper and 7-Up. Shasta was handled out of the San Francisco office. We tried to keep obvious competitors in separate offices, as to reduce any question of a conflict of interest, and our salespeople knew not to share information on their clients with others. We had a very strict policy: if they did share information about other clients, they would be fired.

Just as we gave Coke the same information as we gave Pepsi, we also gave them seasoned, experienced individuals to service their account. But it was up to them to take maximum advantage of the information we gave them to increase their own sales. Coke couldn't afford to let Pepsi get all of the A ads in any specific market, so they didn't ignore our information. Then Pepsi began to get aggressive as well.

My first pitch to Pepsi was back in 1968, when the soft drink giant was head-quartered on Park Avenue in Manhattan. I wanted to talk to their VP of sales because most of the time the sales VP is the person who implements the promotional programs. At that time, the ear I was seeking was Bob Sanders's. I knew Bob from Scott Paper Company in Philadelphia, and had sold him our service when he was the VP of sales there. A few years later he relocated to Pepsi, so I was glad to have an old friend that would soon become a new contract. "So we can review the value, why don't you pick several markets and put some information together," Bob said. "Then come back in and share that with us."

The presentation was made up in Pepsi's new headquarters in Purchase, New York. Donald Kendall, CEO and chairman of the board of Pepsi, and the president, John Sculley, sat in on my presentation, in addition to fifteen or twenty others. They were excited because at that time we were offering them not just data, but also the promise that I'd report back to them on a quarterly basis and make a presentation of the information we'd found. I'd point out to them the A ads that they were getting and we would make sure we covered the competition's activity as well.

At first, I surveyed three markets for Pepsi. Since we were already doing business with Coca-Cola, the information database on carbonated beverages was there for me to analyze. We broke it down by performance over the past six months, then also by region, market, and account.

I showed them the three markets and the information we had gathered and computerized from those markets. We could format it any way a client liked and it would show them what accounts in what market had the greatest potential. I showed them the A, B, and C ads they received in each of the three markets in addition to the ads received by each of the competitive brands. I also explained how the ad classification was determined.

Because they were savvy, the chiefs at Pepsi were able to discern that this was significant information. Of course, they wanted to expand from the three markets I had shown them, Bob Sander told me. At that time MAJERS had fifty markets under analysis.

Pepsi ordered a twenty-five-market study and then I went back and assembled the information and returned to make the presentation. At that time, we were able to demonstrate the A, B, and C ads, the weighting, and their share of the promotional activity.

A simple presentation of facts showed that in one market Coke was outperforming Pepsi with a single act: getting more A ads than Pepsi. In another market, they were holding their own. In a third market, they were outperforming Coke. Sander saw where he had an opportunity.

"I want to implement this with my salespeople," he told me. He took his program and our information and built a system of incentives with his sales organization. It became MAJERS's information, it became the MAJERS system. The goal: to attack U.S. markets that were heavily dominated by Coca-Cola. In the 1970s, Coke's share of the domestic market was estimated at 34 percent. By working together with MAJERS information, in 1977 Pepsi increased its volume of units sold by 11 percent, while Coke only increased by 7.3 percent. In a period of five years, Pepsi's share of the market had grown from 15 percent to 22 percent, giving Pepsi a reason to be optimistic for the future, and Coca-Cola a reason for concern.

■ ■ ■

"I still feel we can be number one," Pepsi's then president John Scully said in the June 12, 1978, issue of *Business Week*. Determined to continue to expand its share of the market, Pepsi's managers constantly made calls to our people to inquire about specific ads. Bob Sander was determined to use feature ad placement to make Pepsi as big a player as Coke was in the retail soft drink market. During presentations, Sander and other Pepsi executives were particularly engaged, eager to know every detail about what ad combinations were running in each market, in addition to the size, displays, and subsequent sales from these features.

Mike Allen took over the Pepsi account at MAJERS from Larry White in September 1981 after Larry was promoted to the newly created position of vice president of marketing. MAJERS's account with Pepsi was $300,000—our company's largest at that time. Mike saw the potential for Pepsi's growth, giving up other accounts to focus his attention on improving their sales performance.

That Pepsi was our biggest client was due, in large part, to Bob Sander, Pepsi's previous VP of sales, who made our weighted index of Pepsi/Coke feature activity a key sales incentive for his team. He included our measure in bi-monthly briefings to Pepsi's chairman Don Kendall, When Ron Tidmore took over from Sander, he was equally focused on MAJERS and feature ads. His sales managers constantly called Mike Allen to question our classification of specific ads. Soon, we were refereeing in Pepsi's hard-played game with an equally tough team from Coke.

In the summer of 1982, at our annual planning meeting to finalize our commitments, Mike Allen presented Pepsi's, and other client's, commitments to the company. During the prior five years, rapid sales growth came primarily from selling new clients. By 1982, we had sold over 95 percent of U.S. packaged goods companies, and Mike believed that future growth would have to come from expanding relationships and revenue with large, sophisticated clients like Pepsi. With the support of Mike's boss, John O'Keefe, he proposed to focus most of his time on the high potential Pepsi account and give up a number of other accounts in his mission of delivering a large sales increase to MAJERS. His strategy paid off.

With the help of our excellent research analysts, Rich Wellen, Kathy Finnegan, and Karen Walsh, Pepsi continued to increase market share in their dogfight with Coke, and within three years our annual revenues from Pepsi increased from $300,000 to more than $3 million.

Allen loved making presentations to the Pepsi Bottling Group, where the company's president, Bob Detmer, executive vice president, Roger Enrico, and their team were intensely focused on beating Coke. One example of Pepsi's attention to detail was when Coke began paying retailers to run multiple package ads, which included combinations of cans and bottles. Pepsi wanted to know *every* detail about these ads—what combinations of ads were running in which markets, and at what prices, and whether Coke was really getting incremental displays and sales from this strategy. Of course, MAJERS could provide all of that information—and more. Encouraged by Roger Enrico, we worked with marketers Frank Wainright and John Voaden to deliver a series of consulting projects using feature ad data, scanner and store delivery records, and in-store display information to understand Coke's strategy and formulate a response.

Of course, we would have done the same thing for our client Coke—if they had asked.

In February 1982 Allen presented the MAJERS system to eight hundred sales managers at the Pepsi Bottling Group Annual Conference in Palm Springs. For most clients, we developed slides at our own expense. But Pepsi wanted all of their presentations to be consistent. When Allen brought his draft presentation to Pepsi's graphic artists, they had been instructed to redesign it as a dramatic five-screen show, complete with special effects. At the conference, Allen was surprised to find that most of the Pepsi senior managers used three-screen presentations—and only the highest officers John Scully and Roger Enrico used more than five. Clearly, features were a hot item for the company! As a result of our presentation, Allen was invited to speak at a similar conference for Pepsi USA, and then contracted to conduct ten regional workshops with their sales teams around the country.

Later in 1982, Roger Enrico was promoted to president of Pepsi USA, and he brought Dan Clark with him from the Pepsi Bottling Group as vice president of marketing. Dan was seeking to increase the intensity of focus in smaller markets, beyond the 106 then tracked by MAJERS. Allen worked with him to develop a custom panel to track another 100 markets exclusively for Pepsi. Closing this sale brought Pepsi's MAJERS account to more than $2 million annually.

Around this time, Pepsi held one of their "Top of the Top" meetings, where CEOs of major grocery chains met with Pepsi senior management to discuss presentations by top people from major consultancies. I was invited to speak at this event and we were able to close the sales of several of our new products over the next few years. After that meeting, I gave Allen some specific actions that I thought would be beneficial for Allen to take at Pepsi. Allen considered them carefully, but decided that my recommendations were not right for the account at that time. I was quite persistent, and we discussed this with considerable energy on both sides. But then I relented and decided to allow the field general—Mike Allen—make the final decision. He later told me that it was a real positive to work for a company where he could disagree with the founder with no negative effect on his career. Of course, Allen was delivering dazzling results.

In early 1983, Allen walked into the office of Joel Mesh, research director at Pepsi USA, and almost tripped over a three-foot-high pile of boxes. Joel told him mournfully that Pepsi had contracted with a vendor to track in-store displays. But instead of getting reports and analysis, they only got reams of raw data. At MAJERS, Larry White and Bob Schmidt were in the midst of developing a MAJERS in-store display tracking service so Allen's interest level in Pepsi's data was high. He asked Joel Mesh to let him take a couple of boxes back to our headquarters and analyze it. Two weeks later, Allen was able to present the analysis of the data to Pepsi's senior management team, which lead to an even larger consulting project for MAJERS.

In late 1983, when Pepsi signed on as the first client for our display service, a key reason was that we had demonstrated our commitment to helping them use information to improve their business. The display contract put Pepsi's account with us at well over $3 million annually. By 1984 our Pepsi account had increased to over $4 million annually and by 1986 we had a $6.5 million contract. As Pepsi pushed for greater growth and success for their operation, MAJERS was equally invested in helping them achieve those goals. The beauty of our business was that the stronger our relationship was with a client, the better results we could likely obtain for both of our companies. Our work with Pepsi became the epitome of a mutually beneficial relationship.

By utilizing performance measurements and monetary incentives for its salespeople, Pepsi was able to overtake Coke at the retail level, though Coke would continue to dominate in sales of fountain syrup. But MAJERS wasn't in the soda fountain business.

■ ■ ■

Our experience was growing along with our bottom line. While we were working with giants like Pepsi and Coke, I figured we needed to educate our clients on the value of our information. That would serve two purposes: it would show people what we do as well as minimize our contract termination. To learn how to best accomplish this, I attended a three-day IBM seminar to educate their clients on the evolution of data processing that was held at their facility in California. I stayed in dormitory-style accommodations, with a single bed, desk, and lavatory. The setting was on the company's privately owned golf course with meeting facilities nearby. The classrooms were theater-styled with tiered seating in a half circle design. The black boards were electronically controlled and the instructors were IBM salespeople. There were charts that showed the evaluation of EDP and projected where IBM would be in the next five years. Their instructors were open and fun, yet very informative.

The first day we went around the room to introduce ourselves and to tell why each of us in the audience, as IBM customers, was in attendance.

"I want to gain some insights into how you run your schools, and then I plan to adopt your methods for our company," I said.

They liked my honesty, and they were very helpful. The instructors explained their program of training, they gave me their class agendas and they told me the dos and don'ts of running a corporate school.

Upon my return, I wanted to create something akin to the IBM seminar for MAJERS.

"This is a perfect approach to educate and stimulate our clients on the use and value of the service we provide," I said to our manager, who immediately agreed. We would call our educational program the MAJERS Marketing Institute—it would be our customer education school, modeled after IBM's customer education seminars.

Gould Flagg, formerly a manager at P&G, and I worked together to develop the final stages of promotion growth. The content for the classroom was designed by Steve Kingsbury, also an ex-P&G brand manager, along with George Beaumont, who had just joined us to run and develop the MAJERS Marketing Institute. (MMI)

Our first class was in Chicago with fifteen client sales and brand people in attendance. That was the beginning of the MMI, which later became an educational forum respected and attended by hundreds of our client's personnel in a non-competitive setting.

They learned how the retailer puts together the specials for the weekly ads, what promotional offers are best received, and how important timing is in the process. They learned from each other the process the manufacturers used in their promotional planning. They laughed at George's golf jokes, had their group picture taken as a remembrance, and left with a much greater awareness and understanding of how the MAJERS information can be used to enhance their promotional effectiveness.

Many contracts were strengthened after attendance—especially by clients who had questioned the value of our service. While MMI was developing, we had other issues to face, something that giants like IBM and P&G knew well: competition.

In 1980, this concept blossomed into the MAJERS Marketing Institute (MMI). If the name "Institute" seems a bit pretentious, let me assure you that a number of executives in the packaged goods field used us as a training school for their own employees.

The original purpose behind MMI was self interest—to teach clients how to use our data to their best advantage. But we expanded to the point where grocery products companies were sending their brand new MBA graduates to our schools to learn about the retail grocery business, something usually neglected at ivy-covered universities.

At the beginning of the 1980s our business was rapidly expanding to the point where our client representatives were busy giving full attention to their customers. As a result, we experienced a cancellation rate I considered excessive. Our original objective with MMI was retention of clients and education of brand managers and field sales managers in the use of our featured data, which was our sole product at that time. At this time, our sales were about $6 million, with a profit of just under $1 million after taxes, and we employed about 260 people. Our cancellation rate on contract business was 12 percent. After two years, the cancellation rate had fallen to 8 percent. The goal was to eliminate the loss of the smaller company contracts that lacked the knowledge of how to employ the information to their benefit, and to expand our business with our larger clients.

We dealt with some market research people who didn't fully understand what we could do for their companies. Upper level management understood the value but didn't always comprehend the implementation or application.

Then, two important changes took place. We started hiring sales people from consumer packaged goods companies to sell our products and services. These people were creative in getting in front of sales and marketing executives who could see the value of our data. They began using this information in their sales presentations to major supermarket chains across the country.

By starting our own institute we'd be able to spend more time with clients, enlightening them on the power of the data. Information was our business so it made sense that we would provide a service that would better enable our clients to understand and apply this information to their business... and to their profit margins. We started the institute on a shoestring, feeling our way through, with two or three different people involved over a period of several weeks. We couldn't settle on what our focus should be.

About that time, in the spring of 1981, I was in St. Louis on other business and invited my old friend from my Brite*Eyes days, George Beaumont, to dinner. I casually asked him how things were going.

"Not so well," he replied.

By then, George was executive vice president of the Rexall Drug Company, which had over ten thousand franchise drugstores across the U.S. and Canada. It was a pretty impressive position, but the company had recently been sold and the new owners installed a new president. George was disappointed with the selection, and before long he was looking for something else to do.

When I told George about the rapid growth that was taking place at MAJERS and the vision I had for continuing to expand the business, he got interested. As the current VP of sales at Rexall and the past director of sales training at Johnson and Johnson, George had always seen the value of quality training and knew the impact it could have on a business. I reminded George about when he was the representative for the public advertising agency in New York assigned to IBM, and he helped me develop my first sales presentation. He looked at me across the dinner table, smiled and said, "You've come a long way, baby!"

I invited him to join MAJERS, but it was a hard sell. He knew Omaha and liked it all right, but he and his family loved St. Louis and didn't want to leave. I coaxed him to come up just for a visit. I told him that coming to MAJERS would be a very challenging but rewarding experience and that I was committed to making it work because I could see the value the educational effort had brought to IBM. I was sure it could play an important role in MAJERS's future. I knew that George had been involved in Toastmasters for a number of years. "You have great public speaking skills and are an exceptional talent," I told him. "Your SRI profile confirms it! I *know* you could make the MAJERS Marketing Institute informative, educational, and fun."

He liked our environment and energy, and he was impressed by the enthusiastic attitude of our employees. He accepted the job, and I turned the Majers Marketing Institute over to him.

We had held our first seminar in May 1981, before George formally joined us. At the invitation of Steve Kingsbury, who was in charge of the MMI Development, George attended the meeting on his own and came away with some ideas that could change our direction and improve the program. He gave us a focus and laid the groundwork.

One week prior, I was in New York with Bill Wyman, one of our sales managers, who was presenting to Colgate. I met with Reuben Mark, the president of Colgate's grocery products division. After introducing myself and thanking him for the busines, Reuben said, "Who is your competition?"

"Our competition is the lack of understanding of the value of our information and how it can help the client improve their sales," I said.

He looked at me and said, "I have never heard an answer like that. What are you doing to resolve that issue?"

I then told him about MMI. "Come with me," he said.

We walked to the sales administrator's office. After introductions, Reuben requested that Colgate send six of their sales and marketing people each to the next four classes at the MMI.

Reuben Mark was an exceptional leader, and is now the CEO of Colgate.

We had a new mission: "To help our clients do a better job of managing their trade promotion expenditures."

After George came to Omaha, we had a strategic planning session for MMI. We used a concept that I had developed called "The Five Stages of Trade Promotion Growth" to position the seminar. Each session began with a study of the Five Stages and how they had evolved over the years. We hoped to educate clients on how the growth of the grocery industry as a whole and how it had changed, and would continue to change, and ways that retail chains and companies should promote products.

The first stage of growth in trade promotion management is a growth in cooperative advertising allowances—alowances given to grocers by manufacturers to advertise their products. Years ago, when retail stores were less corporate and significantly smaller in terms of both floor space and movement of goods, the bulk of promotional monies were spent in advertising alone. As supermarkets became the dominant grocery retailers, cooperative advertising through promotional displays and reduced prices came to the forefront.

By the 1950s, most retailers had headed into Stage Two, which involved growth in volume merchandising, which mean truckloads and traincar loads of prodcut in a single store. The supermarket boom was on, and the industry began to measure success from both a retailing and marketing standpoint. The number of products increased in terms of not only variety, but the shear volume of goods being sold and consumed.

Stage Three involved Target Marketing, where manufacturers sought incremental increase in sales volume, achieved by promoting goods on a market-by-market basis. With the overall product movement throughout the industry at a high, the successful retailer could increase their market share by focusing attention on the differences in individual markets, increasing promotional dollars wherever necessary and eliminating unnecessary spending in other areas—an area where MAJERS's expertise became invaluable.

Stage Four heralded the Systems Approach, incorporating the use of computer technology and changes in the heirarchy of sales positions within a company. In this stage, the sales promotion manager held senior responsibilities, and needed to respond to new data collected through supermarket scanners, or other developments in sales tracking techonology. With a faster rate of return on information, the sales promotion manager could see, and hopefully respond to, changing needs in numerous markets much more quickly than ever before.

Stage Five involve Profit Control, wherein a company could significantly reduce the promotions budget by executing promotions with the most information possible, available through new technology developments and faster transmission. A successful company would need to become savvy in promoting products in different markets with many different competitors.

At that time, most companies were at Stage Three or Four. Only one or two were at Stage Five. There were many interesting discussions on what a company needed to do to reach the fifth stage—the epitome of maximizing the expenditure of trade promotion dollars.

We decided to always have a leading merchandising executive from major supermarket chains at each session as well as other noted authorities in the supermarket industry. We structured the sessions to be fast-paced, with a variety of discussion groups, case studies, and a limited amount of lecturing.

We wanted this to be a learning experience that people would enjoy while also learning new information that would benefit them in their day-to-day jobs. We also scheduled the sessions so participants would have time to socialize with each another and the guest speakers. The focus was on the retailer—the supermarket managers—because they were becoming more and more powerful in influencing the consumer in his or her buying habits.

Kraft was a good example of how our institute functioned. Each year Kraft hired thirty to thirty-five young MBAs right out of school as assistant brand managers. They knew little or nothing about the nitty-gritty of retail selling. In a relatively short time they were exposed to how buying and merchandising decisions were made by retailers, plus they had the opportunity to ask questions and be in the same room with the so-called retail experts.

In two intensive days, we taught them more about the retailer and trade promotion than they could possibly have learned in business school. Kraft's vice president for marketing heard our story and subsequently sent nearly every one of his young trainees, eight to ten at a time, to our Chicago sessions.

In our classes, we talked about what was going on with retail trends, how the supermarkets were gaining control, and how they held the leverage on marketing products because they were the closest to the consumer. These managers were demanding more and more promotion dollars from the manufacturers. The managers were saying, "Don't spend your money on national advertising. Give it to us and we'll spend it on local advertising—some television, but mostly on our weekly newspaper ads. We'll build displays. We'll help you sell your products."

The larger companies continued their national advertising, but the aggressiveness of the supermarket chains was the best way for smaller players to get their products off the shelves and into the consumers' shopping baskets.

Once our students knew what was going on in the retail world, we next showed them how grocers assembled their ads and how they made buying and merchandising decisions. We had a workshop session where each of four teams put a retail ad together, listing the top twenty grocer items featured that week. Then they calculated profitability from the developed advertisement. Then each presented the results and the merchandising strategy that was employed. We covered the way manufacturers could help retailers sell their products, and how to develop a trade promotion strategy. We explained how to implement that strategy, selling the idea to both the retailer and brand manager's own sales force. We provided examples of how to use MAJERS data to accomplish these objectives.

I honestly believe we avoided the hard sell, but our course did give us a chance to show the power of MAJERS data in a subtle way. We worked hard to be as objective as possible. We informed the audience on the true value and appreciation of the MAJERS information.

Among our speakers was a professor from the University of Southern California, who conducted a buying skills seminar for chain store buyers. He spoke to our students on some of the things he was training buyers to do. We always invited a buyer or merchandiser from a major grocery chain to speak. Our institute became a well-recognized forum where marketing managers, product people, and sales and marketing people could learn how to be more effective in structuring their promotion programs and in spending trade promotion dollars. We also spent quality time with supermarket executives and their counterparts from other manufacturers. We tried to not have people from competing companies in attendance at the same session, so that each felt comfortable discussing what their company was doing to promote their products.

At our early day seminars we presented a case history regarding our experience with Hinky-Dinky, the former Omaha grocery chain with forty-two stores, where I'd once sold my Brite*Eyes bleach. It was a good, growing operation, but the name would never be taken seriously by our young MBAs and sophisticated big-city clients. It always brought a laugh at a time when we were trying to be serious. So we dumped Hinky-Dinky as a case history and developed one with Kroger.

I made another miscalculation regarding my hometown. When we built the newest building at the MAJERS headquarters, we included a large meeting room specifically designed for the Institute, with a private lunchroom and several telephone booths. But I never had much success attracting clients to an MMI session in Omaha, and we finally gave up. Instead of asking them to come to Omaha, we went to them.

We were one of the first customers of a new Marriott Hotel in Tarrytown, N.Y., located in Westchester County, where many of our major clients had their headquarters—Nestle, Pepsi, General Foods, and others. It was close to Manhattan but rural enough that after a day of classes our students could play tennis, jog, and swim.

We typically conducted four sessions annually at the Westchester Marriott, two or three in Chicago, one or two in Los Angeles for the manufacturers on the West Coast, one in Atlanta, and others in various cities. Some of those sessions were what we called in-house meetings. We would take our show, for example, to the Nabisco main office to train their people in-house. Those presentations, naturally, were geared to that company's special usage of MAJERS data.

At first, we charged $350 per person for our general sessions, but soon the fee was $850. We had more trouble selling at the lower figure than we did at the higher. When we were newcomers into the training arena, and not everybody was ready to buy our product. But, by mid-1980, we had no trouble attracting clients, even at the increased fee.

We tried to limit attendance at the general sessions to twenty to twenty-five, a comfortable number for breaking into smaller groups. Sometimes, at the in-house sessions, a company would send one hundred people or more, and use the sessions to get their marketing, sales, and market research people to work together to determine how they could do a better job of promoting their products and not waste promotional dollars. Sales and marketing people were perpetually at war with one another, saying, "You don't understand what we have to do to get our products promoted by retailers!" Marketing's focus was on share of markets, profits, and the bottom line, so marketing didn't want to spend any more money than necessary to get their products promoted by retailers. Their main focus was on advertising, a much more glamorous expenditure. Marketing personnel would develop the promotional programs along with the sales managers. The sales organization would then sell them to the retail trade. On another stage, the consumer promotions people would be running coupons valued at fifty cents or more on their own schedule.

MAJERS helped show the way to ultimate benefit. Our information research showed that when a coupon is advertised or made available through the mail on its own schedule its impact upon increased sales is next to nothing. But when tied in with an A advertising feature by the retailer, it will increase the feature impact by another *35 percent*. As an example, normal weekly sales is one hundred units, but with an A ad feature it becomes two thousand units depending upon the product category. With a coupon, the two thousand becomes twenty-seven hundred units. These illustrations and many others were the reasons why it was so important to show this information, but even more importantly to provide a forum where sales, marketing, and consumer promotion could communicate and understand how working together would improve trade promotions spending efficiency.

Most of our speakers would not let us record their talks. "This is off the record," they'd tell the students. It wasn't, of course, but we honored their requests for no tape recorders, which meant George and his MAJERS colleagues had to take pages and pages of notes, from which they would always compile a report to circulate among interested MAJERS personnel. The reports helped our people keep abreast of the latest developments in the retail field, and they also served as the basis for our own critiques of our performance at the sessions. We consistently tried to improve the information we presented and the way it was presented.

At one session, a regional sales manager came late and refused to sit down. He just stood and leaned against the wall. George invited him to sit down, but again, he refused, so George asked him to step outside the meeting room to discover what the problem was. The man told him that he had been traveling for the last two weeks and he wanted to be at home with his family. His boss had called him the previous Friday and told him he *had* to attend this session.

George told him to come in and have a seat, and if by the first coffee break he didn't see any value in the seminar then he could leave and George would would supply an excuse for his boss. At the coffee break, the man told George that he would stay until the lunch break. By lunch, he was joining the discussion, asking questions. By the end of the two days, he told George that those were the most productive days he had spent since he joined his company. He had learned more about supermarket merchandising in those sessions than he had in fourteen years in sales.

At the beginning of MMI, one of the toughest sales was to our own account executives. They were reluctant to promote MMI and didn't see how it could help them. We didn't pay them commissions on MMI sales so many of them saw it as a threat to the clients budget and taking dollars away from the research budget. After a few sessions of MMI that client's people had attended, they were raving about what they had learned and how they had the chance to spend time with a retailer.

George always opened each session with a joke or a story to get people to relax. One of his famous stories was about Arnold Palmer putting on a clinic at a blind golfers convention.

One of the blind golfers, who was an admirer of Palmer, came up to him in the lobby the night before. "Would it be possible to play a round of golf with you?" he asked.

Palmer said sure, but he was puzzled at how blind people played golf. The blind golfer explained, "When you lose one of your senses, the others become much more acute. Since we cannot see, our hearing is more sensitive. We have the caddy stand by the pin and ring a bell, and we aim towards that sound."

Palmer was impressed and asked him what time the golfers wanted to tee off.

"Midnight tonight," was the their reply.

We helped our clients see what we were doing.

MMI taught me a great lesson: In order to get a premium price for your product, you have to look for ways to give your customer added value. In our case, that added value was to *show* them something that helped them be more effective in selling their products. With MMI we were not only able to educate clients on creative ways to use our data to sell retailers, but we exposed their people to key merchandising and marketing executives from major retailers.

I'm a firm believer in education—it's simply impossible to know too much. I'm also a firm believer that if your customer—the lifeblood of your business—is having trouble putting your product to his best advantage, you should not hesitate to send him to school—even if you have to start a new school just for him.

Aisle

12

THE SHELF OF

Good Timing

I didn't want to sell MAJERS. But as I'd done throughout my business career, I never let opportunity slip away.

It wasn't that I especially wanted to sell. I *had* to sell.

Not because we weren't doing well—better than I'd ever dreamed—but because the market was changing, and just as there had been the perfect time to launch MAJERS, the perfect time to sell came on November 17, 1985.

Tom Wilson, a senior partner in McKinsey and Company, was an industry expert whose guidance I had come to rely upon. We met to discuss the business, and he started our 1985 meeting at Chicago's O'Hare Airport with some unexpected news.

"You aren't going to be able to grow this business the way you have been," he said.

I knew what he was saying was true, but nobody had said it in such black and white terms before. "Because the manufacturers aren't going to keep spending the promotional dollars they way they have," he continued.

Manufacturers were consolidating ads by selling volume discounts. As an example, he stated that two clients of ours—Oscar Meyer and General Foods—had recently consolidated, and would soon be saying, "We don't want to pay your fees on both of our brands separately."

Competition was also intensifying; some of the companies were bigger and stronger than we were—and some had been knocking on our doors, asking us to consider a merger.

"You can, of course, stay independent," Tom said in the airport. "But your competitors want what you have and have vastly more money than you'll ever see in your lifetime. They will build their own systems, take some of your better people, and compete with you on price."

If we decided to stay independent, Tom said it would take us seven years to even know if we had made the right decision or not. Seven years of struggle, as the bigger companies, which we'd spurred, would be raiding our systems, customers, and personnel.

I must have asked a million questions. "Should we go public?"

"No," Tom said. "Even (the advertising agency giant) Ogilvy Mather couldn't make it work."

"What about passing the company over to someone else?"

"It's difficult to pass ownership," he said. "You should consider selling now, rather than after you are gone."

I returned to Omaha and relayed Tom's suggestions on to top management, as well as the board. I got all the marketing people together, and what they said surprised me.

"Let's go with somebody who has deeper pockets!" said about two-thirds of the management team. "We can make it work."

I went with the majority.

"We'll open our doors to the people who have been wanting to merge with us or buy the company," I told my staff. "I just want you all to know first, because I have never operated in anything but a forthright way with you."

■ ■ ■

"How much do you think the company is worth?" I asked Joe Konen, our VP of finance, who was one of the many people who streessed that we were ripe for a sale.

For me, selling MAJERS was no different than the other products I'd sold in my career, outside of price, of course.

First and foremost, you have to understand the needs of your prospective buyer. I outlined in the opening chapter of this book how our product lines in the packaged goods promotional field provided an excellent fit for those who wanted to buy us. The clients wanted all the information available in the promotional field, and we offered the most concentrated information of any of the players in the market research business. Our suitors needed us, they needed our database, our excellent employees and our excellent management, so we were lead to believe.

In the credit analysis field, Dun & Bradstreet is the expert. Dun & Bradstreet is almost a generic term, growing at 15 percent per year.

Likewise, in our segment of the marketing information field, MAJERS was the generic term.

We were a perfect match. Now, all we had to do is to show them that the merger was meant to be.

Our team was ready: Dick Patterson and Joe Pfeister of Touche-Ross; our attorney, Ron Parsonage; Allan Macklem, our treasurer who worked on the due diligence study; and, above all, Frank Schanne, my executive vice president and COO, plus the people of our marketing department who helped me make the original decision to listen seriously to our suitors.

All of us, from time to time, would spend hours talking about how we should package our sales information and what the price should be. Some outsiders could take a look at MAJERS and offer $30 million, while SAMI had offered $12 million. But it was up to me; I had to decide the price. It really hit me one day when I heard Joe Konen's magic words:

"If you're selling, it's worth $45 million. If they want to buy, it's worth $65 million."

■ ■ ■

Sixty-five million dollars. It sounded right. The discounted cash flow formula showed a high of $85 million. Sixty-five million was a fair price for MAJERS. All I had to do was sit back, not panic, and make the other side realize that they wanted to buy.

The board felt our justified max sales price would be around $45 million. But Joe's advice stuck with me: I didn't want to sell, not until somebody wanted to buy. We met with the Touche Ross accounting firm in New York where their chairman, Grant Gregory, listened to us tell about the success of MAJERS. He liked what he heard, especially about our long relationship with Dun & Bradstreet/A.C. Nielsen. He suggested we stress that relationship, however possible.

We began working in conjunction with Braxton Consulting Group in Boston, owned by Touche Ross, to assemble a formal presentation on the company's position.

I learned a lot during this period, especially how a discounted cash flow formula of evaluation worked. As Laird said, the lower the cost of money, the higher the value of the company and vice versa. As the formula states, cash flow discounted by the cost of money (10 percent interest, plus 3 percent inflation, plus a 2 percent margin) over a projected five-year period will yield a higher price—versus using a cost of money that totals 20 percent, which will give you a lower price.

After a preliminary meeting with Time, Inc., I went to Nashville, Tennessee, to visit with the CEO of *Southern Living Magazine*, a recent acquisition of Time's. He shared his insights and confirmed the value approach of using after-tax profit margin as a multiple of revenue. I remembered what my trusted advisor Ted Laird had told me: "Remember, 6 percent equals one times revenue and 18 percent equals three times revenue. In a service business a good rule of thumb in selling a business is: Bottom line net profit of 6 percent of sales will justify a sales price of one times annual sales revenue. Twelve percent will justify two times revenue."

We stayed with the goal of seeking approximately double our annual revenues as a sale price. Hardly anybody ever tells you about this simple formula, which would mean not $45 milion, but $65 million, a fact that I discovered over lunch with Jed Laird, of the investment firm of Hambrick and Quist, where he told me the formula that would change my life and the lives of my employees

"This formula will hold true right down the line for a service company," Jed said.

When our board member Willis Strauss heard I would be meeting with some high-powered folks from New York—five of them from Time, Inc., including Dick Munro, the highest name on the masthead of every Time, Inc. publication; the chief of SAMI, their warehouse withdrawal research arm; plus a couple of other executives including Jerry Levin, he also had some good advice:

"You will be asked two questions before serious discussion begins. First, 'Have you come to the point of at least being receptive to selling?' Second, 'What are the four or five key factors that are important to you, factors you will demand satisfaction on before agreeing to sell?' Give those questions serious thought. Be prepared with your answers."

The New Yorkers from Time, Inc. came to Omaha by private jet and were welcomed to our new executive headquarters offices. We gave them a tour of the facilities, including the MMI seminar room, the vast computer center, and my office. Because I always wanted to make my visitors feel at ease, I never used a desk with drawers and side panels and my office was large and comfortable. At this meeting, I joined the visitors in sitting around the coffee table. After a cup of coffee and a few social exchances, we got down to business.

When Dick Munro, the head of Time, Inc., and his entourage settled down to business, one of the first things out of his mouth was almost exactly as Willis Strauss predicted:

"Have you come to a point of at least being receptive to selling?" he asked.

"Yes, I have," I replied, following the script I'd rehearsed.

"What are the four or five factors that are important to you, factors you will demand satisfaction on before agreeing to sell?" he asked.

I pretended to ponder that question; but, of course, I had rehearsed my answer. "My four concerns are: We must remain in Omaha and be given enough autonomy to run our own business. Our people must continue to have the opportunity to grow and develop. MAJERS must continue to have a commitment to this community. Money is number four: We must come to a fair and equitable financial arrangement."

Munro turned to his associates. "Anybody have trouble with those?" he asked. None did. We were underway.

The next step: We flew to New York, where the expectations of TIME's marketing division, SAMI, wined and dined us during the next two days of meetings, most of which ended at Le Cote Basque restaurant. Halfway through the filet mignon I was finally asked what we would want for MAJERS, but I dodged a firm commitment. I did say something to the effect that, when A.C. Nielsen was sold to Dun & Bradstreet, the price was twenty to twenty-five times earnings. (A.C. Nielsen sold for 1.6 or 1.7 times revenue since their margin was 9 percent.) I did not mention the figure $75 million (twenty-five times our $3 million), but simple arithmetic would lead them to that number.

Maybe I was too coy, not coming right out with a figure. But this was early in the process and Time/SAMI was our first persistent suitor. When C.C. Daniel, president of SAMI, asked during dessert if we would sell for fifteen times earnings, I continued to demur. I wanted a formal offer, not a conversation over dessert.

We returned to Omaha. One week later I received the supreme slap in the face from Daniel: a letter offering $12 million. I took the offer to the board and they agreed with me. The offer was an insult, not even worth a reply.

Time wanted our management team, but I wasn't going to let them steal it. Later, instead of buying MAJERS, SAMI bought Burk Marketing in Cincinnati, and from there went downhill rapidly. TIME eventually sold off the division to Control Data and recently IRI purchased the SAMI customer business.

Things went better in our negotiations with our second suitor: IRI of Chicago. They flew some people to Omaha and were impressed by our operation. All our relations with them were friendly and their offer came close: $62 million.

But they wanted more of a merger than a sale, with us receiving stock instead of cash. I frequently awoke in the middle of the night, thinking about what would have happened if I would have accepted their offer in light of the stock market crash of October 1987. In the end, we cut off negotiations, feeling the fit wasn't right and that, if anything, we had more sophisticated management than they did. We later learned IRI had been trying to sell their business to Dun & Bradstreet, which would be our third suitor.

The call came from someone at A.C. Nielsen, the Dun & Bradstreet subsidiary, and I told them I'd be willing to listen. Then, I waited. Nearly four weeks passed before they called again. Apparently, they were doing a deep backgrounder on us, discovering what our clients and competitors thought of us. The investigation, I learned later, was done by Bain & Associates, a consulting firm out of Boston that had an unusually close relationship with Dun & Bradstreet. I learned that at almost every level of management in Dun & Bradstreet's business, a Bain consultant sat beside the Dun & Bradstreet manager. It was sometimes hard to tell whether decisions were from D&B or Bain.

But we couldn't have been more pleased with Bain's findings than if we'd hired Bain ourselves. They spoke to marketing directors, research directors, and sales directors. The overall evaluation: "Positive." Their production evaluation: "High quality data," "Sets the industry standard for trade promotions," "Reliable."

Procter and Gamble's reps told Bain, "MAJERS has the most professional and the most knowledgable people of anyone that calls on us. They know the true meaning of customer service. You should approach them for an acquisition. Their people will be a great asset to Nielsen."

Matters between A.C. Nielsen and MAJERS turned serious. We dealt with two layers of executives: most from Nielsen, who were not experts on how we could fit snugly into their operations, and those of Dun & Bradstreet, who were street-smart in business acquisitions. I think the Dun & Bradstreet team realized that Nielsen's management, successful as it was, needed to be jolted into a full state of awareness. We'd always considered them a bit stodgy, sleepy, and not too hard to outrun if we really hit our stride.

Mostly, we negotiated the potential sale ourselves. We did have excellent help from several people at Touche Ross, including the firm's executives Grant Gregory and Dick Patterson. Before he had become the chairman of Touche Ross a few years earlier, Grant was my neighbor in Omaha. He introduced us to Braxton Consulting in Boston, which worked with us on our sales strategy booklet.

Before walking into the lion's den of negotiation with Nielsen, Dick Patterson, Joe Konen, and I talked out our strategy. We decided that I would be the nice guy and Dick the villain. If we needed some emotion to get them off the dime, Dick would provide it. He knew a few words more often indigenous to the barracks than the executive suite. And he was ready—and eager—to use them.

I was the one who would put his arm around my counterpart from their side and invite him into a side room for a little quiet, dignified discussion. "There isn't anything gentlemen of good will cannot settle amicably," I rehearsed saying.

■ ■ ■

The night before our meeting, we stayed in the Waldorf Astoria, right next to the Dun & Bradstreet offices. At 9:45 a.m. we packed up and headed to our 10 a.m. meeting. We were greeted by their negotiating attorney and their CFO. "Good morning gentlemen and welcome to Dun and Bradstreet," said the CFO, leading us into the conference room.

Introductions were exchanged, coffee was served. We then entered the exchange, discussing the discounted cash flow approach to valuation. Dick Patterson asked the first question. "Please explain your determination for the cost of money," he asked. "How did you come up with 20 percent?" They were reluctant to get into the details. That was when Joe Konen put up the transparency showing the detail of how we arrived at 14 percent.

"The cost of money is 9 percent, the inflation rate is 3 percent, and 2 percent for cushion. Now, with that as a guideline, show us how you arrive at 20 percent."

Their CFO was still not willing to get into the detail. I figured this was because we differed on how much we thought the business was worth. They thought $45-50 million, while we were at $65-70 million.

After three attempts, Patterson, with some very colorful language, insisted upon an answer. Believe it or not, we were all shocked to hear a CFO of a major corporation respond with, "That is the number they told me to use."

You can imagine what hit the fan. After that, we were solid with our presentation justifying our value. Their attorney, Peter Lessler, was not budging. He was a good negotiator and I knew he wanted a deal to be consummated. "Peter, let's you and I go down the hall to a side office," I said.

Peter agreed. "We both want this to be successful and your management along with Bain, the consulting team, knows this will complete your strategic grid for promotion evaluation," I told him. "Tell me what we need to do to arrive at an equitable cost of money? This business is the best acquisition prospect you have been involved with. Bain told us that. Our accounting is honestly presented, our people are the best of the best, our information is uniquely valuable, as our mutual clients have told you. I won't sell this business for $50 million. So it is important you come to our aid and help to get this done. Think about that and we can meet next week in Northbrook."

I knew my points were well received by Peter, and the meeting was concluded.

Having a savvy ally like Touche Ross would be well worth whatever fees we paid, especially Dick Patterson. He was relentless, even, at one stage of the negotiations, forcing a financial "expert" from the other side to admit he didn't really know his numbers.

Under Dick's questioning, it became clear that, as a second-level executive, the stand-in had no flexibility to meet offers with counteroffers. He had been told by his superior exactly what to do and what to say. When his rote statement of an offer failed to impress us, he was at a loss.

With that, MAJERS was able to move in with authority and set the tone for further talks. We had the advantage. I had never been down that path before, but other associates had. Touche Ross knew the moves.

It pays to go with the pros when you're entering an unfamiliar field.

D&B's board of directors was meeting to decide whether on not to provide the money to buy MAJERS. We knew we couldn't attend that meeting, so we did the next best thing: we controlled the agenda by assembling a concise booklet that showed how MAJERS could best complete Dun & Bradstreet's jigsaw puzzle of services.

We pointed out that the marketing process for today's consumer products could be divided into six major activities: product development, advertising, distribution, promotion, consumer research, and market share. "Manufacturers today spend billions on the marketing process and are interested in the effectiveness of each activity," we wrote in our booklet. "And in recent years consumer package goods manufacturers have come to recognize the growing importance of trade and consumer promotion.

"Different market research companies, such as A.C. Nielsen, IRI, SAMI, and MAJERS, provided partial solutions to the manufacturer's desire to measure the effectiveness of all of its activities."

"The merger of MAJERS and A.C. Nielsen would create the first single source of marketing information for use by sales, marketing, and research departments in consumer package goods companies."

We were able to provide such a convincing presentation because of a lesson we had learned long ago: Know your competitor. Know what he does best and worst. I think we knew Nielsen better than Nielsen knew us, and that helped us in the negotiations. Never did we feel intimidated by the company, even though they were far bigger than we were. Because the only way to compete with a giant is to have as much, if not more, information than they do, and then to set the agenda yourself, instead of following their's—and, of course, information was our business.

Nielsen's president, Dick Vipond, was involved in most of the discussion, but the details of preparing for meetings was handled by his representatives, and attorney, Peter Lessler. Peter was an expert, nearly unflappable. He knew what D&B wanted to pay, and he was honorable in his efforts to serve his company. He was tough, and we respected him.

Joe Konen, our CFO prior to joining MAJERS, had been involved in the sale of A-C's electrical products company to Siemens of West Germany and the construction machinery unit to Fiat of Italy, each of which was worth in excess of $100 million. At the time Peter Lessler was meeting with us, he was in the middle of six major deals. But, he told me, the other deals were smaller.

"It's different negotiating for an entrepreneur who owns and controls the company," Joe said. "You get quick responses, but you are also dealing with an emotional issue. There is very little emotion in a large corporation."

After we'd proven to Dun & Bradstreet that we added real value to their company, both through our booklet and in our meetings, we began negotiations. I had very specific objectives and I refused to give up much maneuvering room on the essentials. I wanted the $65 million. I wanted a management bonus pool of $5 million to retain key managers at MAJERS. I wanted D&B to buy my building for $4 million, and I wanted to remain as CEO so I could personally focus D&B's attention on the excellence of our performance. I was prepared not to sell MAJERS unless my terms were met—and I let them know it.

The secret of negotiations, of course, is to get more than you give. We would give Peter Lessler eight discussion points, perhaps three of which might be meaningless to us—points that we would give up in order to get others.

Peter was using the same strategy, always striving to avoid coming down to a single issue, because if it's a difficult one, there can be no trade-off. There is nothing to trade. Matters get too focused on the single issue and resolution becomes dangerous, if not impossible.

Peter was a great "waiter," and I don't mean the kind that brings your dinner. He would wait, and he was more comfortable responding to our position than he was in stating his position. But there is value in waiting until someone states a position. Then you can modify that position. A more active style of negotiating is not unique, but it is different from the textbook style.

Our goal was to try to reach a point where everybody wins.

Once D&B decided they wanted to buy MAJERS, they got down to the final sticking point: *price*. Peter Lessler started out in the high $30s, low $40s.

We responded not with $65 million, but higher, $80 million, justified by the discounted cost flow formula.

Peter was figuring slightly more than 1 times revenue, which for the previous year had been about $33 and was expected to reach $35 million for 1986. The $65 million was 1.9 times 1985 revenue. I thought we could command that figure because we were in the marketing information business. Had we manufactured widgets, a fair price might have been $20 million to $30 million.

I thought we were on our way. But then, as things do in marriages and mergers, everything fell apart.

■ ■ ■

It was in the middle of a meeting in Northbrook, Illinois, Nielsen's suburban Chicago headquarters. We sat at a big rectangular table, our people on one side and theirs on the other. On our side were Joe Konen, our CFO; Ron Parsonage, our legal counsel; and me, as well as Dick Patterson and Joe Pfeister of Touche Ross. Peter Lessler and Dick Vipond led their side along with the D&B finance VP.

I thought we were going to do the deal right then and there, but then somebody from their side asked if we were going to structure the deal as an asset purchase or a stock purchase.

"A stock purchase, of course," I said.

"No," they replied. "Our intention is to buy the assets."

They wanted not only the value represented by our stock, but also our assets, cash, furniture, equipment, and inventory.

"It is not a very important point, but from an acquisition standpoint it's critical," they said. "It has a lot to do with how a deal is structured, and how the taxes would be paid."

Included in the purchase of MAJERS was the sum of $6 million we had in the bank. Peter Lessler and DickVipond wanted another $3.2 million to satisfy the tax issue.

Prior to 7 p.m. when the Dun & Bradstreet people, as the hosts, brought in some sandwiches, which looked pretty unappetizing to us, and we decided this was a good time to caucus. Several issues remained to be resolved, but the $3.2 million was the overriding one.

There was silence.

They were looking for us to make a counter offer, but we weren't going to do that.

More silence.

Finally Dick Vipond broke the deadlock.

"I'm going to overstep Peter Lessler and I'll probably get in trouble with Dun & Bradstreet, but maybe we can split the $3.2 million, at $1.6 million apiece," he said.

We suspected this was part of their act, all staged. Peter Lessler was the main negotiator, and DickVipond couldn't have taken over without prior agreement. It was a concession on their part, but it left me short of the $65 million I felt we deserved.

I sat there without saying a word for what seemed like an hour. It was actually about two minutes. Sweat was beginning to pop out on foreheads all around the table. Still, I said nothing.

Finally, I suggested that we break for the evening. "We're not going to come to a conclusion tonight," I said.

We picked up our papers and went off to dinner. Since Dick Vipond was flying out of Chicago early the next morning for a meeting, it appeared that further negotiations between MAJERS and Dun & Bradstreet were very far away.

Over dinner that night, we made up our minds to meet with Peter Lessler one more time. Everybody else was leaving for home, but Peter planned to stay until the next afternoon. Joe and Ron canceled their morning flights to Omaha to have one more go at it.

I had an engagement at Creighton University in Omaha that I did not want to miss. Before going to bed I called Dick Vipond at home at 11 o'clock. I asked him honestly: could he come up with any additional monies? He said he'd given his last dollar and if we were to receive more, it would need to come from Peter Lessler. He suggested we let Joe and Peter meet once more in the morning.

"Could we meet D&B's terms and still come away with the $65 million we wanted?" I asked.

I thought we could find the extra $1.6 million in MAJERS's accounts receivable, which we could add to the $6 million already in retained capital.

We agreed we probably could find the money somewhere, and Joe was given the go-ahead to see how the other side felt about this solution. The next morning Joe met with Peter Lessler, offered the $7.6 million in cash, along with the stock and our assets, and the deal was on again.

The final negotiation point was A.C. Nielsen's purchase of our new headquarters building. The closing was set for December 18, 1986.

Back in Omaha, the additional $1.6 million turned out to not be much of a problem according to Allan Macklem, our treasurer and VP in charge of accounts receivable. Nabisco owed us in the neighborhood of $2.5 million and was a little slow in paying. Allan offered them a 2 percent discount for an immediate settlement of the bill, and Nabisco quickly sent a check to our bank.

Of course, all of this financial maneuvering on our part hadn't been completed by the meeting time the next morning, but the plan was in motion and we felt confident we could accomplish it. We'd given D&B the extra cash their people wanted, and we got the sense we had achieved our goal of $65 million. But, of course, I didn't know whether or not the deal would be done when I left Chicago.

I knew it had possibilities, but wasn't sure how Peter Lessler would react.

By late afternoon, Peter had completed a a four-page letter of intent that, in essence, settled all the areas of disagreement. This was not the slam dunk, end of negotiation, deal-is-done moment. Sometimes, when you try to put on paper the things you have said, the meaning gets twisted. But they kept at it until they were in accord.

Joe and Ron Parsonage were the MAJERS reps left in Chicago. I jumped into an airport limousine and hurried to O'Hare where I was getting to the plane to Omaha. When I arrived for my afternoon meeting I was told, "You have an urgent phone call."

I grabbed the phone with my heart in my throat.

"You have a deal. We have the verbal agreement for $65 million in cash."

I'd been waiting nervously all morning, and when I heard the good news about 2 p.m., I think I might have actually broken down and cried with joy and pride at the accomplishment.

Everybody was happy. D&B ended up getting the additional $1.6 million. I had the satisfaction of receiving the full $65 million. I had my heart set, and wouldn't settle for a $63.4 million check. They got the additional cash for the tax payment, but receiving the full amount we had fought so hard for that meant a great deal to me.

As always, a good deal is the deal that's good for both sides.

■ ■ ■

We held our own celebration at the office the next day. Final papers were signed later, and on November 24,1986, *The Omaha World-Herald* ran a story under the headline: "Omaha Market Research Firm Sold."

"MAJERS Corp., an Omaha company that turned a simple idea into a nation-wide business with annual sales of $35 million (for 1986), is being sold to Dun & Bradstreet Corp. for $65 million, the two companies said Monday," the article read. "A.J. Scribante, who started MAJERS in 1963 with $500, will continue to run the company, which will be operated as a separate business under Dun & Bradstreet."

On December 18th, we set up satellite dishes at each MAJERS office location in Stanford, Chicago, Atlanta, San Francisco, and Cincinnati so that they could share in our announcement program. In Omaha alone we had four hundred employees, family members, board members, civic leaders, the MAJERS management team, and executives from Dun & Bradstreet. In the satellite offices, we had another two hundred employees that were part of our celebration. We taped the entire program.

I announced the final stock value.

"Now then, to reflect back on the stock value for the past two years, in 1985 our stock value was $34.75. In 1986 it had grown to $54.60—a nice 57.8 percent gain. Our sale price for the stock comes to a gain of 232.6 percent, or $127.00 per share!"

The cheers went up, the applause and excitement thundered across the MAJERS organization. Our employee stockholders got a large dividend for their hard work. The profit sharing was increased, and our stock soared.

We were not just a bunch of bumpkins from Omaha. We were a sophisticated team of professionals. We stood up to the big boys from the Windy City and the Big Apple, and we had gotten our price.

THE SHELF OF

Moving Forward...

As I write this, I am chairman and CEO of a company called Vital Learning Corporation. Its headquarters have been moved from New York City to Omaha, and its business is to sell training programs to other companies.

This transition came as somewhat of a surprise. When I sold MAJERS Corporation, I never anticipated being involved in another business venture. But I was fifty-six at the time of the sale and too young for the rocking chair. I had assumed I would continue as chief executive officer at MAJERS, which would operate as an independent entity under reasonable control from Dun & Bradstreet.

I was wrong. Nothing worked out the way I envisioned. We believed we were selling an organization to D&B. What they bought, in their eyes, was a database, a product line. They didn't perceive buying a growth-oriented business with people who were capable of doing exciting and profitable things. They didn't perceive buying people who had a mission, people who would go forth to solve the problems of the promotional expenditure dilemma.

We started with great anticipation, great desire, and a lot of confidence that D&B's top executives planned to live up to their word. I told Charlie Moritz, their CEO, that I wanted this transition and acquisition to be his finest. In my opinion, we could have done many great things for D&B, but they were not in tune with us. Many of the A.C. Nielsen managers were threatened by our marketing people.

I was upset, and the reason stemmed from an incident involving one of our clients. Then, on the day we were closing, something strange happened. We had put a proposal before the client that called for a fee of $120,000. It was brought to my attention by our client management representative that reps from A.C. Nielsen had approached this same client with a proposal they could deliver for $30,000. The price differential was ridiculous. They intended to provide only data and a bare minimum of service, rather than our extensive, high quality service. Yet Nielsen had name recognition and a reputation based on television viewer marketing surveys. We discovered later that their accuracy reading was *67 percent* vs. our prideful 99.9 percent.

On closing, I immediately requested a meeting in our Omaha office with Jack Holt, the executive vice president of Dun & Bradstreet, and Dick Vipond, president of A.C. Nielsen.

"What's going on?" I demanded of Holt and Vipond. "If you leave your proposal on the table, we're going to lose business and our sales person will lose the commission. We won't be able to service the client to the maximum because we can't afford to put our people against your unrealistic offer."

They both backed down. "We will withdraw and let your people take the customer," Holt told me. "We'll go with your pricing schedule," added Dick Vipond.

I was never one to demand that every oral commitment be reviewed by an attorney, put in writing and signed by all concerned. Maybe I should have. We continually had to fight the battle of Nielsen competing with us on price alone. Time after time, Nielsen people undercut our pricing format. As a result, they became a head-to-head competitor of their own subsidiary, MAJERS. Can you imagine? Buying a company and then competing against that company? It made no sense to me, until later.

Jack Holt had also upset some of our executives in another way. At the closing, he stood up in front of our people and promised that he would come around and greet every one of us. He never did. He ignored my top people, and they were disappointed. They wanted to be appreciated in the executive suites of their new owners. It was D&B's largest acquisition, but the CEO, Charlie Moritz, never made a sincere effort to welcome our people to the D&B "family"—which was shocking considering how close the MAJERS family had become.

Further, as vacancies occurred at Dun & Bradstreet, they raided MAJERS to fill the holes in their staff. Prior to our closing, D&B had instituted an early retirement program, which they never told us anything about, and which created a number of openings at the top levels. Naturally, some of our best people wanted to capture those opportunities, and the D&B executives encouraged it.

But part of the sales agreement called for a one-year earn-out proposal. We sold the business in December 1986, but the agreement was that the better our performance in 1987, the higher the final purchase price would be. We focused on having our best year ever in order to boost the selling price, thereby rewarding our stockholder-employees. But D&B's raid of our executive corps began to hurt MAJERS's business. They could have waited until after the earn-out period before offering jobs to MAJERS executives, or they could have informed us and worked together with us to resolve the issue.

They didn't wait, and I'm convinced we lost a few million dollars on the final price as a result. In the first quarter of 1987, I finally challenged them on their hiring practices, telling them they had overstepped their bounds. I told them they had violated our contract by talking to our people about their opportunities.

I shared with them a letter I planned to send to all our clients informing them of our planned action, and to let them know that under terms of the sale MAJERS was not merged into Nielsen, but was supposed to be a free-standing company. I showed Holt and Vipond a draft of the letter I planned to mail and, again, they backed off and said they would stop their raids and protect our earn-out agreement.

I can't fault the MAJERS people who got D&B jobs with greater responsibility. But I do fault Dun & Bradstreet for not respecting the terms of the sale and keeping MAJERS strong. Dun & Bradstreet's proclivity for bureaucratic management did not change just because they now owned a company with "people" managers. So one day, after one of D&B's management conferences, I wrote a six-page letter to Charlie Moritz, explaining the difference between our system and his, and suggesting he adopt portions of ours.

You know what? I never got a reply. He never said, "I'm the boss!" He never said, "You're full of you-know-what." He never said, "Don't ever write another letter like that to me." Just nothing.

As we approached the end of the first year, again in the face of reassurances that Omaha would remain the home office of MAJERS, A.C. Nielsen tried to transfer nearly a dozen MAJERS executives to the Nielsen home office in Northbrook, Illinois. A number of them refused, resigning from MAJERS and embarking on other ventures in Omaha and elsewhere. It turned into a real disappointment, and A.C. Nielsen/Dun & Bradstreet and our mutual customers were the losers.   Around this time, I saw Dick Schmidt, D&B's executive VP of finance and administration with Dun & Bradstreet, at the cocktail party in Carmel, California, for D&B annual leadership conference, which included executives and the operating presidents of each company and division. Dick complimented me on the high caliber of our people at MAJERS and indicated that D&B was counting on us to do some great things for their corporation.

"We ensure the success of our people," he said.

I asked him how he did this.

"By not providing them with the room to fail," he said.

The answer astonished me. "How can you provide people an opportunity to succeed without at the same time giving them the room to fail?" I asked.

He didn't have an answer.

I thought about his comment over the night, and the next day when the two of us were in a workshop session, I gave Dick my analysis of the situation. "It seems to me that by taking the approach that D&B takes, you are communicating to the employees that you do not trust them," I said. "And the reason, in my opinion, that you do not trust them is because you do not know them as thoroughly and as objectively as you could. You encourage your people to mistrust themselves even though not intentionally, and at the same time, to learn to trust the policy and procedure book."

"This is bureaucracy at its finest," I said.

Dick said it was interesting insight and certainly worth thinking about. I suggested that we begin to alter the culture of the company in such a way that it could bring about trust in each other and in my opinion, form a stronger foundation for the ensuing competition, which existed in each of their divisions.

At one point Jack Holt asked me to come to New York to get involved in D&B's human resources department. I suppose he realized what a fine job we had done with the selection and management of our people. I turned him down. I had no desire to report to Holt. I never felt he personally intended to do anything to hurt MAJERS, but I did think that he wanted to get our price lower than the negotiated sale price, by hurting our 1987 performance against the earn-out.

Twenty-five years of MAJERS information was incorporated into the Nielsen Master Data Base, becoming part of their integrated intelligence made available to their clients, which were also MAJERS clients. The transition took more than a year to complete with the Nielsen account staff having the advantage, even though their knowledge of the promotional process was limited. A few of the MAJERS client management personnel remained and made significant contributions to the Nielsen organization. However, most eventually left, one to become president of the corporate division of a Fortune 500 company, another to become a management consultant, another to open his own headhunter firm.

Their culture was bureaucratic and limiting to the growth of our group, whereas our culture had always been personal. We gave our people room to succeed while simultaneously giving them room to grow.

The lesson learned? When you sell a company, walk away. Be happy. Don't expect the same respect for your people's talent and abilities that you gave to them. Your people will not have the opportunity to raise the level of the acquiring company's performance. Instead, they'll be lowered (or risen) to the acquiring company's performance and culture.

■ ■ ■

When the wire transfer was complete, I phoned my friend, Warren Buffett.

"What do you do with capital such as this?" I asked.

He suggested I read two books, *The Intelligent Investor* and *You Only Have to Get Rich Once*. The second book was out of print so he loaned me his copy.

"You might consider putting some money into Berkshire-Hathaway," which is, of course, his phenomenal investment fund. I read both books and invested over a million into Berkshire-Hathaway in December of 1987.

Both the books and the investment paid off phenomenally.

My three-year contract called for me to remain with MAJERS until at least December 1, 1989. I was eager to leave before then, but they didn't want to make the announcement of my departure. They finally agreed to my early departure— and on December 1, 1987, I left, after twenty-three sometimes-challenging but always stimulating and rewarding years on the job. During the few remaining months, I concentrated on working in community affairs. But something was missing. Well, *everything* was missing. So, on January 1, 1988, I formed a new company, whose purpose was to seek out and buy a new business. I decided if there was no longer a place for me at MAJERS, I would turn my energies and enthusiasm down new avenues. Two of my former MAJERS associates joined me in the new venture, which we called, VITAL combining "vision" and "talent," and decided on a set of criteria to be met by the new business we would purchase. It would have to meet all these criteria before we would consider it:

-We wanted to sell the product to a white collar decision-maker.

-We wanted the average sale of our product to be $25,000.

-We wanted a quality product we could be proud of.

-We wanted a rich market so we could grow the company at a fairly good pace.

-We wanted to show at least a 25 percent return on equity.

-We wanted to be able to manage a direct sales force vs. sales agents.

-We wanted a mission within the company.

-We wanted to be able to buy the company at a fair price.

Sticking religiously to those eight points, over a period of fourteen months we investigated three thousand companies, seriously considered two hundred of them, and became involved in the financial statements and due diligence studies of a final twenty. Of that number, we found the jewel that met all our strict standards: the training division of McGraw-Hill Publishing Company

The company came to our attention for the first time in November 1988. Our management team spent a very busy holiday season and winter going over McGraw-Hill's facts and figures. We came away highly impressed with the company's opportunity and the integrity of McGraw-Hill. We bought the business in February 1989.

McGraw-Hill had operated its training division for about a dozen years. We acquired one hundred associates and employees with the purchase, and we have already made a few changes in personnel in New York City and San Diego, our two largest operations. We have a very small executive staff in Omaha: Dave Erdman, our president and chief operating officer; myself as chairman of the board and CEO; George Beaumont, our executive VP of sales; and Jim Howe, our executive VP of finance who is also involved with our military business.

Our first decision was to call this business VITAL LEARNING Corporation. We engraved the sign on the door at our headquarters office in the Regency district of Omaha.

VITAL LEARNING Corporation sells pre-packaged training products. We teach people how to sell, and we can teach them how to sell *anything*. We can train a person how to sell IBM computers or how to recruit sailors for the U.S. Navy. There are twenty modules in our customer-oriented sales training package, including such topics as how to find prospects, how to make the presentation, how to fulfill the customer's needs, how to close the sale, how to handle rejection, and how to come back strong for the next potential customer. When Nippon Telephone and Telegraph in Japan came to America to find the best sales training program, their extensive research brought them to VITAL LEARNING. We put together a contract and they became our distributor in Japan.

VITAL LEARNING provides workbooks, video tapes, and audio cassettes. If a business has its own training officer, VITAL LEARNING will teach that person how to make the best use of the material for his company's sales force. If the client isn't large enough to have its own training officer, VITAL LEARNING will provide a trainer to teach the course. These various courses are also available online for the most efficient method of training people located in the world.

VITAL LEARNING's mission reads: "Building our clients' profits through the training and motivation of their human resources to deliver legendary customer service."

VITAL LEARNING doesn't limit itself to teaching a single kind of training. We are concerned with training a client's employees to be the best they can be, and to maximize their productivity for their competitive advantage.

At MAJERS, we were selling the client an information system on his promotion effectiveness, and again at Vital Learning, we're a partner with the client.

Our customers include many of Fortune 500 companies as well as several smaller businesses, the U.S. military, a number of secondary schools and colleges, universities, and a variety of other private businesses. Our potential is to serve every company in or out of the Fortune 500. We don't have all of the Fortune 500 yet, but that is the beauty of a rich market.

As *Forbes* magazine reported in its April 25, 2005, issue, "The broker A.G. Edwards, which invests 6 percent of payroll in employee training has, over the past five years, easily beat the S&P 500 and the average brokerage. The typical firm invests 2 percent of payroll in training."

Some executives aren't convinced training is productive or they worry that workers will leave for higher pay once they have been trained. At MAJERS, I found the opposite to be true. The more we invested in our people, the more loyal they were and the greater productivity we received as a result.

We have added one hundred-fifty independent sales agents, something the company didn't have under McGraw-Hill. They will focus on the top one hundred companies in the U.S. We also have an international division, which totals about 10 percent of our business. We operate in Japan, Taiwan, Canada, England, Australia, Germany, Mexico, and France. All our training lessons are in the native language.

In May 1989 we established a distribution and customer service center in Omaha, consolidating inventory from New York state and northern California for better control and to take advantage of the central location for shipping purposes. Our sales representatives work freelance—in Dallas, Chicago, Salt Lake City, Atlanta, New York, Indianapolis, Tucson, San Francisco, Cleveland, Kansas City, Omaha, and in Washington, D.C., to name a few.

We've been asked how long it takes to train a person. Our answer: "An indefinite period." At IBM, for example, sales people never are considered fully trained. They learn from the day they come to work until retirement. Training is an ongoing process. That is part of the potential of VITAL LEARNING. It's not a case of training a client and then moving on. A client may remain a client for years.

So far VITAL LEARNING has avoided teaching the specifics of an industry, concentrating instead on universal sales techniques, but there is potential for that kind of specific training. We would have to add specialists in a variety of fields—education, banking, insurance, hospitals.

So I've changed course, embarking on something different. It isn't new as a business, but it is new for me. We expect VITAL LEARNING Corporation to grow by applying the same principles of business I employed at MAJERS.

■ ■ ■

Speaking of MAJERS, the company finally slid into the dreaded bureaucratic phase of management, where policies—not people—run the business. We sold them an organization, but they only wanted our database. It's their prerogative, of course, but I believe our people threatened Nielsen's organization and they never even had a chance to perform. A.C. Nielsen did value our production operations and executives like Jim Howe; they retained about two-hundred employees who stayed in Omaha, where they reside to this day. Our marketing people departed one by one.

MAJERS was an unlikely but phenomenally successful company, founded with $500, a good idea, great timing, and a bedrock belief in its people as its primary asset. It lives on in the memories of those it employed and served.

THE SHELF OF

Extraordinary People

Herewith, thoughts from a few of the people who helped make MAJERS great. Our success, and this book, would not have been possible without them.

"B.L. Byars, one of the few people who was at MAJERS before me, once said the company 'survived and grew because of A.J. Scribante's extraordinary luck, dogged persistence, stubborn determination, and unmitigated gall.' I would disagree with none of that, but would add the characteristic I consider most important, his unwavering faith. An entrepreneur must believe he will succeed—that faith lies behind, and enables the passage through, all the dark and difficult time. You can be at the brink of despair, or bankruptcy, or collapse from exhaustion, but you go forward if you believe success lies ahead."

—Warren Conner, Director of Special Services

"At MAJERS I learned the power of bringing excellence in service to our clients to help them make intelligent decisions concerning their trade promotion expenditure. I was able to recruit some of the best sales talent from the best companies because of the opportunity we could offer people to be part of building a dynamic company.

—Frank Schanne, retired COO

"Perhaps the greatest lessons I learned from my very enjoyable days at MAJERS was to invest the time, no matter how long it takes, in selecting your staff and treating your associates as your most valued resource. When you have the right people, and meet their needs, you have a winning team. "

—Jim Howe, retired Air Force Lt. Colonel–VP Mastertrack Production

"MAJERS was the best collection of talent I've ever been associated with, and that includes companies such as Pepsi and Reebok. A.J. had a gift for identifying talented people and motivating them to produce extraordinary results. One of the greatest lessons I learned at MAJERS was how to be comfortable with top corporate executives in selling value added services and strategic concepts. "

—David House, General Manager, Stamford office

"The underlying principles at MAJERS were rooted in quality and value. Nowhere was this more significant than in the selection of people. Although tempted to fight the selection process, in the end, the discipline was rewarded many times over. I learned it was far better to invest in finding top talent rather than suffering through managing those without . . . After a particularly frustrating episode, A.J. told me, 'I'm not very tolerant, but I'm eternally patient.' I've found immense value in this principle."

—Allan Macklem, retired Air Force Lt. Colonel–Controller

"Majers was a great learning experience for me and many of the things I learned there I have applied at NFO:

The importance of recruiting the very best talent available—and not compromising before you find the right people.

Developing support systems to insure people can perform at their highest levels.

Creating a recognition system that motivates individuals.

These principles I learned at MAJERS have enabled NFO to generate the highest margins in the industry and build a quality organization that is the leader in its field."

—Larry White, VP Marketing

"Many things contributed to MAJERS success as a company-strong customer service, an insistence on having the best products in the industry, and a strong work ethic. I think, however, that the most powerful factor was the quality of MAJERS people. "

—James Vanderholm, VP Operations

"The greatest thing I learned at MAJERS was how to sell...The sales talent MAJERS people possessed was unbelievable and, as we worked together, we learned from each other. "

—Marty Mulholland, Marketing Manager

"We came from various backgrounds but found common ground in our ability to deliver a valuable product to our customers. While the concept was A.J.'s and the demand was high, it was the people that made MAJERS a success. I feel fortunate to have had the opportunity to work with all of them."

—Gary Parkhurst, General Manager, San Francisco office

"MAJERS was the best experience of my life...This association allowed me to develop planning and goal setting disciplines that have enhanced my career in the retailing business. "

—Ray Johnson, VP Technical Services

"I enjoyed the challenge of increased responsibilities each of my seven years at MAJERS. I experienced the frustration of occasional failure (the dreaded lost contract), but, through willpower and management support, I focused on the long term and ultimately enjoyed some success. MAJERS was a remarkable environment that thrived on energy and success. "

—Phil Huber, Marketing Manager

"MAJERS was a unique place. With A.J.'s leadership and direction, it provided an environment that challenged everyone to perform to the best of his or her ability."
—George Beaumont, VP, MMI Director

"There will never again be a better group of performers assembled for the purpose of helping organizations operate more effectively."
—Bill Wyman, Marketing Director

"I count myself fortunate to have been part of this incredible team. I still talk about MAJERS often and find that I carry a piece of it with me every day."
—Sharon Janel, Chicago Office Manager

"MAJERS was the dynamic company that allowed me to make some mistakes, grow with it, and achieve a personal sense of accomplishment far beyond monetary rewards. "
—Dick Chamberlain, VP Quality Control

"There was a unique group of people, working together as a team, pulling together to reach common goals. The company grew into the premier provider of management information data by developing the skills and talents of diverse individuals. We were on the leading edge because we all had a commitment. "
—Bob Finochiaro, VP Operations

"A.J. never made a promise to me he didn't keep—I trusted him, he trusted me. I gained a lot of self-confidence at MAJERS. "
—Marge Behn, Supervisor, Mastertrack Production

"The real story of MAJERS is not the dramatic growth charts or the sales achievements, but the people and the personal growth that took place. John O'Keefe was a great recruiter and demonstrated a rare ability to relate to clients. Bill Wyman, Dave House, and Rich Olson all shared knowledge unselfishly, even as we competed. And our staff in Omaha, including Paul Lewis, Ray Johnson, Red Byars, Bob Finnochiaro, Darlene Fox, Warren Connor, and Jim Howe, were always ready to help, even when we blew away our revenue plan and drowned them in business they had not budgeted to handle. It was a special time.

"When I worked for A.J. at MAJERS, I questioned a few of the decisions he'd made. Now that I'm in my own business, he looks even smarter than before."

—Mike Allen, General Manager, San Francisco office

"An entrepreneur who owns and operates his own business, someone like A.J. Scribante, needs outside directors in the worst way. Fortunately for MAJERS, A.J. is one of those unusual people who solicits and listens to the advice of others. A.J. picked people who had absolutely no interest in being directors of MAJERS, other than providing useful and valuable help, and—this is important—seeing that this help was utilized. He selected people who were successful, financially and otherwise, people who found no ego trip in simply being directors of MAJERS. The company was able to marshal a group of very talented people who not only sold the client on the value of MAJERS' services but then regularly helped them understand it and use it. This gave MAJERS a tremendous price leverage and was the key to its success."

—Richard A. "Dick" Westcott, Director

"I must say I was a little curious about serving on the board of a privately held company. I had never been approached before and I was intrigued. I had spent my entire career in a publicly owned company where we had to think about the stockholders, and the bondholders, too.

"I learned MAJERS board meetings were no different from those I had previously attended. MAJERS would have had to spend tremendous amounts of capital to compete with the likes of Time Inc., and Dun & Bradstreet. The other directors and I could see the changes in the industry because we were looking at it from arm's length. We pointed that out, and to A.J. this was like saying, 'We want you to get rid of your family.' This was his family. It took him a while to agree he'd better pursue it. Then when he mentally crossed that bridge, he did pursue it in a most professional manner. There is no question this was a very successful sale.

"After the sale, while A.J. and his associates were investigating other business possibilities, we once cautioned him not to spend too much money in the search, and then the McGraw-Hill opportunity came along. It was a perfect fit. MAJERS provided a service, and VITAL LEARNING provides a service."

—Willis A. "Bill" Strauss, Director

"I have known A.J. for twenty years, and I think he asked me to join his board because he thought some of the knowledge I had acquired in starting a business might be helpful. There were a lot of similarities. We both started with nothing, and he used my experience in organizational and personnel matters. He has done a fantastic job of identifying the problem of employees. He is very good with people.

"He didn't always agree with us members of his board, but it's my impression he always paid attention. He was always open to suggestions, open to criticism, new thoughts, and ideas. I never kept score, but on balance I'd say he accepted the recommendations of the board far more often than he rejected or ignored them.

"He encouraged participation in every way. It's most unusual that he would pick a board like this one and use it. But, of course, if he didn't use us we'd have all walked away.

"I was chairman of the board's compensation committee, and we discussed A.J.'s salary and bonuses just as a publicly held board would do for its CEO. He provided us with the information we needed, and we talked about it with him and made recommendations. We recognized it was his baby and he could do as he wanted, but invariably he followed our recommendations."

—John E. Cleary, Director

"A.J. had a growing company that was small but successful. I thought he could improve sales and profitability by changing the manner of ownership. I was anxious to see how such a change would actually impact the company. It turned out to be a very good change, with sales and earnings increasing dramatically.

"As a chief executive officer, he had two talents that are very unusual. One, he had a rapport, a relationship, with his employees that was extremely close and personal. He was very effective, much more than the average CEO. He created strong loyalties to him among his employees, and he was loyal to them. This attribute would be hard to fake; in A.J.'s case it came from his heart. He would involve himself in every facet of the employee's life, try to help them in any way he could. This was clearly a strength for him as a CEO.

"Second, A.J. is absolutely a super marketer and salesman. He's one of the best I've ever seen. When employing those talents—his closeness to his employees and his sales expertise—he is nearly unbeatable. I think those are the two main reasons for his success. That would be true whether he was managing MAJERS or any other business."

—James L. Koley, Director

■ ■ ■

Through these extraordinary people and others, I've learned the lessons that built MAJERS and a lifetime.

They include:

Always do what is right and always be honest.

I learned this from my parents, who stressed it from Day 1.

When you show a sincere interest in another person, they will in turn give you respect and support.

The navy afforded me the opportunity to experience this valued lesson.

Listen to others and learn from them . . . Go outside for advice.

This adage began for me in college and continued throughout my life. I've grown greatly from adherence to it.

Why go to work if you can't have some fun at the same time?

It was only when I began down the path of growing MAJERS that I stopped working and started having fun. You'll know when this happens. Keep searching, and working, until it does.

Nothing has a value until you give it a value.

I learned to price our product and service based upon value and not upon cost. More than anything, the value we brought to the client was the value of our people.

Hire the best.

Once I learned the value that extraordinary talent brings to the customer service equation, the door of growth and opportunity opened wide—thanks to SRI and their amazing interview process.

Focus on growth.

Growth is what helps each of us achieve our potential. And as it's often said, "Growth comes from challenge, not from comfort."

*Ego and courage are powerful forces, and that combination, along with other bal-
ancing talents, can achieve excellence beyond your expectation.*

I surrounded myself with a rare caliber of people and we achieved performance
known only by a very few exceptional achievers. Best of all, we had fun doing it.

You build the organization, and the organization will build the business.

When people love what they do and they have a commitment to a mission, good
things result. The competition for accomplishment is exciting and dynamic.

Creative thought is an act of faith.

I learned to believe and I discovered that God never failed me as long as I was
adhering to the first lesson of doing right and being honest.

ABOUT THE AUTHOR

A.J. Scribante is the founder and was Chief Executive Officer of MAJERS Corporation, a national marketing information and consulting firm employing 600 people. MAJERS was headquartered in Omaha, Nebraska, with marketing offices in Stanford, Connecticut; Chicago; San Francisco; Cincinatti; and Atlanta. MAJERS was dedicated to the mission of serving Fortune 500 clients by providing analysis of the effectiveness of promotion expenditures.

A.J. Scribante negotiated the sale of the business without the involement of an investment baking firm. The Board of Directors recommended a sale of $45 million but the ultimate sale was made at a value of around $65 million.

Mr. Scribante is presently the Chairman and CEO of OTTO J Investment Management, a company dedicated to the mission of maximizing investment returns while pursuing both growth-oriented equities and developing companies. He has served on two Public Corporation Boards, the Consultation Committee of STRATCOM, and presently serves on the Eisenhower Foundation and the College of Business Advisory Board at Kansas State University.

INDEX